17th Sept 1999

For Hugh and Ann
With best wishes,
Patrick

Childhood Lost

A boy's journey through war

PATRICK GIBSON

First published 1999 by Patrick Gibson
37 Vivian Way
LONDON
N2 0JA

Copyright © Patrick Gibson 1999

The right of Patrick Gibson to be identified as the author of this work has been asserted by him in accordance with the Copyright, Designs and Patents Act 1988

All rights reserved. No part of this publication may be reproduced, stored in a retrieval system, or transmitted, in any form or by any means, without the prior permission in writing of Patrick Gibson, nor be otherwise circulated in any form of binding or cover other than that in which it is published and without a similar condition including this condition being imposed on the subsequent purchaser

ISBN 0 9536443 0 8

Produced in Great Britain by
Axxent Ltd
The Short Run Book Company
St Stephen's House
Arthur Road
Windsor
Berkshire SL4 1RY

*To my dear wife Janette
and our children
and a special thanks to my
mother Charlotte
without whose help
my early life
would not have been told,
nor chapter 19.*

CONTENTS

Introduction		7
Chapter 1	Beginnings	9
Chapter 2	I return home	19
Chapter 3	Penang to Bangkok	29
Chapter 4	Bangkok	37
Chapter 5	Sumatra	47
Chapter 6	Highlands School	55
Chapter 7	Scouts	63
Chapter 8.	Holidays in Siam	71
Chapter 9	My last holiday in Siam	83
Chapter 10	War in the Far East	91
Chapter 11	Out of Sumatra	97
Chapter 12	India	103
Chapter 13	Journey to Naini Tal	115
Chapter 14	Hallett War School	121
Chapter 15	The Forest	131
Chapter 16	Holidays in Naini Tal	139
Chapter 17	A letter from the dead	149
Chapter 18	ss Otranto	161
Chapter 20	Footnote	181

INTRODUCTION

What I am about to relate covers six years of my life, from the age of nine to fifteen during the time of the Second World War. For most of these years I was separated from my parents and brother, living in Sumatra and India, while they were detained in Siam. There were times of great joy, but also of extreme sadness. I had no roots and was often lost in an adult world which I found difficult to comprehend. I can recall only a few episodes in my life up to the age of six and am indebted to my mother, Charlotte, for filling in some of the gaps which form the introduction of my story.

While my children were still at school I would occasionally tell them of incidents that happened to me while I was growing up in the Far East. The differences between my early life and their own seemed to interest them a lot and I kept on being asked to write down all I could remember from the past. Then in November 1995 I visited the Imperial War Museum to view the Commemorative Display of the plight of POWs and Internees held by the Japanese in World War 2. My interest was to do with internees held in Bangkok, Siam and Kaban Djahe, Sumatra.

Unfortunately there was nothing relevant in the display but, an attendant suggested that I go to the Reading Room. While there I was asked if I would write down everything I could remember of the years I was in the East as it would be a useful addition to the library. So that now I am retired and have time to spare I have decided to put pen to paper.

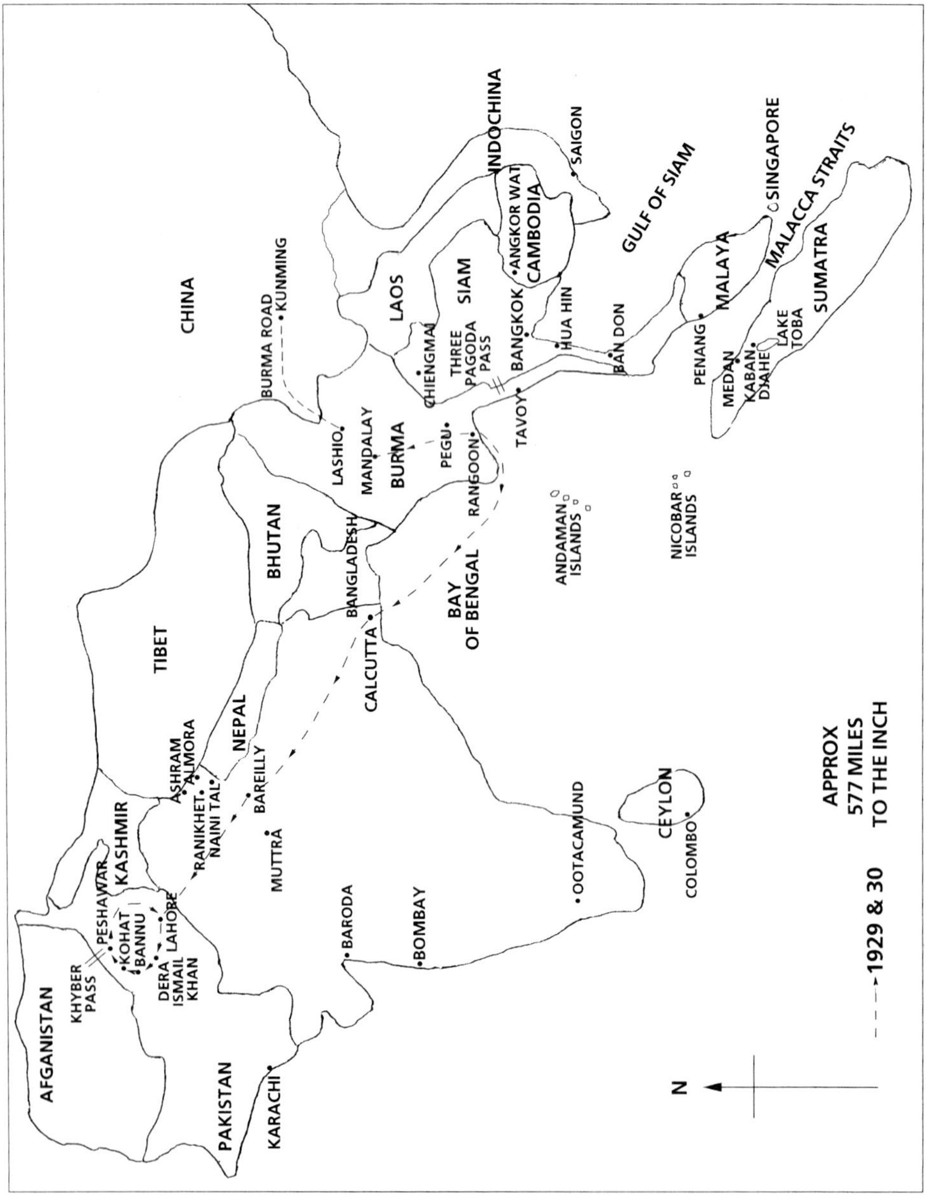
CHINA
BURMA ROAD
KUNMING
INDOCHINA
SAIGON
ANGKOR WAT
CAMBODIA
GULF OF SIAM
SINGAPORE
MALACCA STRAITS
LAOS
SIAM
BANGKOK
HUA HIN
BAN DON
MALAYA
SUMATRA
PENANG
MEDAN
KABAN DJAHE
LAKE TOBA
CHIENGMAI
THREE PAGODA PASS
TAVOY
LASHIO
MANDALAY
BURMA
PEGU
RANGOON
BHUTAN
BANGLADESH
ANDAMAN ISLANDS
NICOBAR ISLANDS
BAY OF BENGAL
TIBET
NEPAL
CALCUTTA
ASHRAM
ALMORA
RANIKHET
NAINI TAL
BAREILLY
MUTTRA
KASHMIR
PESHAWAR
KOHAT
BANNU
LAHORE
DERA ISMAIL KHAN
KHYBER PASS
AFGANISTAN
PAKISTAN
KARACHI
BARODA
BOMBAY
OOTACAMUND
CEYLON
COLOMBO
APPROX 577 MILES TO THE INCH
1929 & 30
N

Chapter 1

Beginnings

My mother clearly remembers that on the night of my birth, someone, somewhere in the distance, was playing , The Birth of the Blues. Before the night was out a storm blew up with thunder and lightning and driving rain, perhaps an omen of my early life. A month after my birth in a nursing home, at Walton-on-Thames at 2 a.m. in the morning of 25th October 1928, my parents, taking me with them, set sail on a P. & O. liner, the journey taking five weeks to reach Rangoon. I was to spend most of my childhood in the Far East in Burma, Siam, (now Thailand) and Sumatra.

My parents had married a year before at the Holy Trinity Church, Brompton, London and my father, a chartered accountant, was unable to get a job at the time of the depression. In desperation and much against his will he joined the Bombay Burma Trading Corporation Ltd. who sent him to Rangoon to sort out their financial problems. On arrival in Rangoon the Company provided a house and father settled down to his new job.

At the same time as we arrived in Rangoon my grandfather, on my mother's side, Colonel J. Fuller-Good was a director of the Indian Medical Service stationed on the Northwest Frontier between Afghanistan and Waziristan, now part of Pakistan. As a young doctor he had assisted the wounded in China during the Boxer Rising in 1900. Now as a surgeon he would tour the cantonments – tending to the sick and severely injured – of the makeshift medical facilities in the Khyber Pass. He was also responsible for, and in charge of, hospitals in Peshawar, Kohat, Dera Ismail Khan including most of Waziristan. In March, April and May of 1929 and 1930 my mother and I, together with my ayah, visited him for holidays. In the mountainous region of the Khyber Pass the weather was cool during these months whereas in Rangoon daytime temperatures could rise to 104°F.

We sailed from Rangoon in a boat of the British India Line down the Irrawaddy River then north to Calcutta. From Calcutta we went by train to Lahore. Although most comfortable there were no corridor carriages which meant that passengers either took meals with them or got out at a station and made their way to the restaurant car returning to their own compartment when the train stopped. On both occasions our compartment consisted of two bunks, one up and one down for mother and ayah and a cot for me. Father had had a box made of teak at the Rangoon saw mill which held a kerosene burner, fuel, and plenty of food, enough for the journey. At Lahore we changed to a single track line to Dera Ismail Khan on the banks of the Indus River. It was a narrow guage line and the carriages were most uncomfortable with wooden bench seats. The journey to Dera Ismail Khan took all night and all day. On arrival we stayed with my grandfather for much of our holiday. His house was made of mud, with a roof of straw and mud. Across the ceiling of each room stretched a very large strong sheet put there to catch the rats that fell through the straw. Hyenas howled all night long which made sleep difficult. When my grandfather had to travel further afield, my mother, ayah and I were taken by car to Kohat via Bannu. We stayed overnight at Bannu which frightened mother as the native Pathan tribesmen detested the British. They are tall, bearded and very fierce; sometimes they would capture a soldier or a white women and keep them hostage as a bargaining tool. The road from Dera Ismail Khan to Kohat was more like a track and at times precipitous. My grandfather would meet us again, at Kohat, where my mother's brother, Larry, was stationed. (At the time Larry was a Flight Lieutenant in the R.A.F.)

In all the train journey took three days from Calcutta and a further two days to reach Kohat by car. The return journey was much easier, driving from Kohat to Peshawar, then catching the train back to Calcutta.

During my first three years of life only two things happened that are worth recounting. As a baby I was exceptionally good, sleeping the night through without waking. My mother became suspicious, as some of the children of her contemporaries were having terrible nights. I was being cared for by a Burmese ayah, that is, until one night my mother caught her administering opium to me, which she had secreted under her fingernails. She was dismissed on the spot. After this my mother had bad nights.

In 1930, when we were living in Burma, there was a severe earthquake with the epicentre fifty miles north of Rangoon, at a place called Pegu. At the time, my parents and I were living in Rangoon at one of the Bombay Burma Trading Company houses, normally occupied by the burra sahibs. These houses were built to withstand earthquakes and were hardly affected except that the bars across the windows of my bedroom had broken loose. The next door neighbour was thrown out of his bath by the severity of the quake. Pegu was reduced to rubble with fires that continued to burn for several days.

The day after the quake I made my way upstairs to my bedroom and finding the bars had been broken, climbed on to the window-sill which overlooked the garden. Below, my father was washing his car, a black Austin saloon. Calling to my father I shouted, "Daddy I can fly!" and jumped out of the window. Apparently I landed in a rose bush which helped to break my fall, but my tongue was badly cut and thorns caused some lacerations, the scars from which are still just discernible.

While in Burma we stayed in Bassein, Maymyo, Mandalay, Ayutthaya and many other places. Once in Mandalay we visited the magnificent oriental palace that was the home of King Thibaw and Queen Supayalat from 1878 to 1885. British soldiers of the time used to call her Queen 'Sour plate'!. Between them the royal couple revived the tradition of the 'massacre of the kinsmen,' killed their enemies, mainly princes, princesses and their children, and had their bodies trampled into the ground by elephants. As a consequence the British deported them to India and later annexed Upper Burma. which became a province of India. After King Thibaw died in India, Queen Supayalat returned to Rangoon where she lived out the rest of her life in a rather drab little run down house and where my grandfather used to attend to her health. The palace was destroyed by the Japanese during World War two.

In March 1932 the family returned to England on leave. It was company policy to allow six months leave after serving abroad for three years. We stayed at the Cotmandene Hotel, Dorking. In November of the same year my father was posted to Bangkok in order to sort out the financial problems of the Bombay Burma Trading Corporation in Siam. We sailed on the Rotterdam Lloyd liner, Dempo, an unusual ship as it had square portholes.

Palace and Home of King Thibaw and Queen Supayalat in Mandalay

BBTCL house, Rangoon, where I fell from upstair window

Cotmandene Hotel, Dorking

Nothing of any importance appears to have happened during the next three years apart from the birth of my brother Jonathon on 1st September 1933, in Bangkok. For a while we went to Chengmai, where the company trained and kept its elephants. We also went to Hua Hin for our holidays. Most of my time was spent in the Royal Bangkok Sports Club, swimming, or more correctly, dog paddling.

November 1935 saw the family returning once again to England for further home leave. We spent two weeks in Swanage where I managed to go over the handlebars of my bicycle and grazed both knees very badly. In January 1936 my parents placed me in boarding school in Sussex and in July my parents and Jon returned to Siam.

Uplands School

January 1936, and I was not to see my parents for the next three years. During term time I boarded at a preparatory school for boys up to the age of nine and girls to twelve. It was called Uplands School, Heathfield, Sussex and although I have returned to

Heathfield I have been unable to find any record of where it was situated.

The school was approached through a large wrought iron gate, past the gatehouse where the Headmaster and his wife lived, along a gravel drive to the front door of a large, rambling Victorian house. The gatehouse was typically Victorian. Inside the lounge, the walls were covered with dark oak panelling. Large heavy furniture stood on a dark red carpet and there were long dark velvet curtains that reached the floor. On two of the walls hung pictures of very distinguished looking gentlemen while the remaining wall supported two shot guns, and what I was told was an elephant rifle, together with two crossed swords. Behind the curtains were french windows to the garden.

At most the school had about 100 pupils. At lunch we had to eat everything that was put in front of us; as I detested all school meat it became quite a problem. Every day saw me alone, except for a master, who made sure I finished the meal. The master would cajole and threaten dire consequences and when this had no effect would turn and look out of a window. It was then that I took the opportunity of stuffing any remaining meat into my pockets which was later disposed of in the flower beds. He probably guessed what I was doing, but was only too glad to get the meal over with.

During the Summer term in 1936 the school suffered an epidemic of whooping cough, a complaint that I had had when much younger. Until it was over, I was billeted out on a nearby farm, which I really enjoyed. The farmer was a large, gruff but very kindly, grey-haired man and his buxom wife an excellent cook who baked her own bread and cakes. The farmer taught me how to milk the cows by hand, find and collect the eggs laid by his chickens and ducks, and to do many other sundry jobs around the farm. Breakfast was a wonderful meal consisting of bacon, eggs, fried bread, sausages, tomatoes, mushrooms, finished off with thick slices of toast and homemade marmalade. Each loaf of bread was enormous and stood about a foot high from the table top but, amazingly they didn't last long as we all had huge appetites.

During the summer term the boys were expected to play cricket, which I enjoyed so long as I was bowling or batting but not otherwise, as I soon became bored. I have a good eye for most ball games and used to play cricket for the school 1st Eleven when there were matches against other schools. It was on one of these occasions at the end of the summer term, that I was supposed to be fielding out at the boundary but instead was chatting to Fay Williams. Suddenly she said, "Look out." As I turned to see what was happening the cricket ball hit me in the eye, smashing my glasses. I had to go to hospital to have the glass removed.

Fay's parents were next door neighbours to mine in Bangkok but were now back in England on leave. My mother had asked them to call at the school to make sure that I was well and lacked nothing. They must have told my parents of my accident as mother sent a telegram to the Headmaster enquiring if I was now quite better and whether it had affected my eyesight in any way. I did not see or hear from Fay or her parents again until I returned to Bangkok but they probably telephoned the school to see how I was after the mishap.

Holidays in England

It was during the Easter holiday of 1937, when staying with my grandparents in Bayswater, that I contracted measles. I was put to bed, curtains drawn and my grandmother bought me a selection of books to read. I was not ill for long but, once better, I found that my eyesight had been badly affected. The optician said that I should never have read and it took three weeks before I was better and even then I had to wear dark glasses for a further month.

Holidays in England were spent mostly with my grandmother and step grandfather on my father's side, my real grandfather having commited suicide during the Russian Revolution. My father and his younger brother were born and brought up in Russia, until father was twelve. His father worked as an engineer in the cotton mills set up by Lord Addington in St. Petersburg and they lived in a grand house on an island in the River Neva. Shortly after the Russian Revolution started they decided to leave, but on reaching Poland my grandfather commited suicide by shooting himself. Why he did this has never been made clear, but he may have been depressed at losing his job in St. Petersburg. My grandmother, who always had great presence of mind, fled to Switzerland, with her sons. Eventually she married Raymond Hubbard a brother of Lord Addington and they settled down in Bayswater in later life.

My main recollections of holidays at Bayswater are of being thoroughly bored, and spending a lot of time sailing boats on the Round Pond in Hyde Park. A mechanical wind-up steamer sank the first time out but was recovered by a man in high boots. It never worked again. Returning home one day with my grandmother I was teased by a bigger boy which infuriated me to such an extent that I lost my temper and knocked him to the ground. The boy's mother was livid and called me a bully and accused my grandmother of being unable to keep me under control. So I was given a severe ticking off but, once we returned to the flat, my grandmother said, "If he teases you again hit him even harder."

In 1937 I spent the summer holiday on the Isle of Man with friends of my parents who were home on leave. One day I decided to ride a cow, so climbing the fence I succeeded in dropping on to the back of an unsuspecting cow which immediately bolted from fright. I hung on for as long as I could, but soon found myself on the ground. My parents' friends, who saw the incident, were not amused and I was shut in my bedroom with curtains drawn for three days and given only bread and water as a punishment.

During the three years away from my parents there was only one holiday that I really enjoyed and that was with my uncle Larry and his wife Joan. Uncle Larry, my mother's brother, was a pilot in the R.A.F., now a squadron leader and based at Duxford. He was the only person who encouraged me to be myself. At school I was frequently ticked off for not behaving and I exasperated my grandparents.

In September 1938 I did not return to school at the beginning of the winter term but, joined my mother's father (Col. J. Fuller-Good) and his wife who had by now retired and had a house in Fleet, called Kinsale.

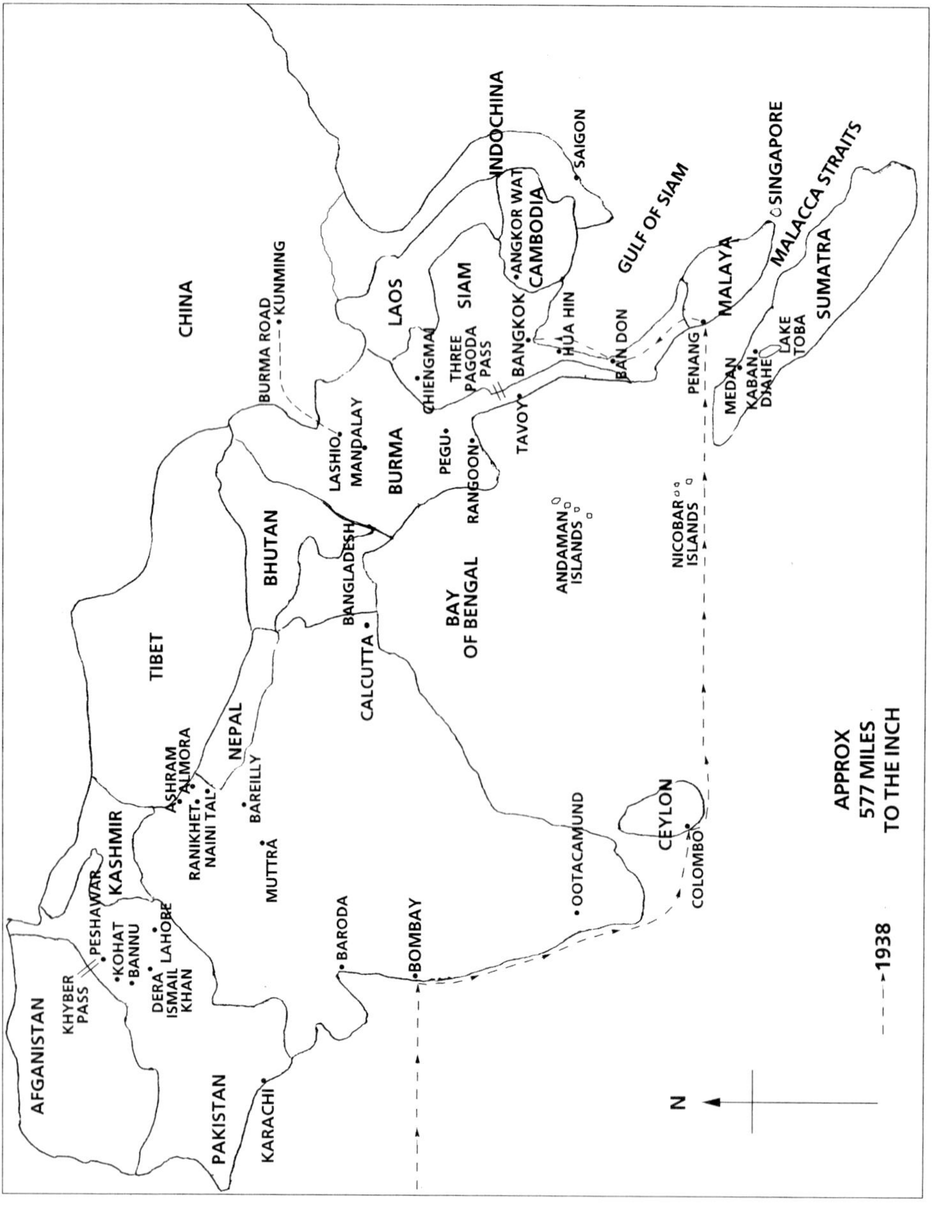

Chapter 2

I return home

October 1938. The calm before the storm. 'French without Tears', London's longest run was still showing at the Criterion. Ivor Novello`s 'Comedienne' with Lilian Braithwaite was being performed at the Aldwych theatre. At the Palladium, Flanagan and Allan were part of a cast of 80 performing 'These Foolish Things'. The Old Vic was in dire trouble as the Underground to Waterloo Station had been closed. Danielle Darrieux was all the rage at the cinema. 'Snow White and the Seven Dwarfs' was showing at The New Gallery Cinema. All lighthearted with not a care in the world. Or was it that only the very few were prepared to face the threat that lay ahead in less than a year's time, while the masses were not inclined to think about the future while they could enjoy the present?

For me whose 10th birthday it would be at the end of the month, life was exciting. I had left boarding school and all I could think of was the sea voyage ahead and seeing my parents for the first time in three years. But what was to follow could not have been predicted.

Outward bound

I awoke early, excited at the prospect of sailing to the Far East, where I was to rejoin my parents. My trunk, a large, solid curve-topped box with strengthening wooden struts was already packed. It would be placed in the ship's hold while I had a suitcase for everyday use in the cabin. The day was breaking but, despite the dreary weather, I was impatient to be on my way. Soon I heard a rustling downstairs and knew that my grandfather was clearing the grate of last night's embers, watched by Jumbo his faithful cocker spaniel. I jumped out of bed and quickly dressed. Grandfather was very tall, well over six feet, slim, but well built with a moustache and silver-grey hair. He had spent most of his life in the Far East. In recognition for his services abroad he was awarded the title of Honorary Surgeon to King George V. His first wife died young, but his second wife, Madeleine, I was to see again after my eventual return to England.

It was the 7th October 1938. After breakfast my grandfather and I went for our usual walk over the fields with Jumbo. Normally Grandfather took his 12 bore shot-gun, but today the weather was too miserable. The countryside around Fleet was almost bare apart from a few leaves that the October chill had not yet plucked from the trees. There was no let-up in the grey, damp weather. I knew the walk well as we had taken the same paths so often before. Jumbo remained obediently at heel; he was now getting on in years and only came to life when his master was out shooting. We walked for an hour and a half before returning home by a roundabout route. I occupied the time before lunch alone in my room speculating on the journey ahead, whether I would recognise my parents, what the ship would be like, would the voyage be pleasant and a variety of other thoughts, flashed through my mind but never remained long.

It was not until after lunch that we started to load my luggage on to the back of Grandfather's new Armstrong Siddeley. The car was two shades of green and looked as though it had been carved out of a block of marble. The trunk secured with rope, a quick cup of tea and we were off to London and to King George V Docks. The weather was still bad and as we approached London it became foggy. It was dusk before we finally reached the quayside. Visibility was poor and although the street lights were on it gave an eerie appearance to everything and sounds were muffled by the fog. I got out of the car and looked up at the liner which seemed enormous to me. On the newly painted hull was the name ss Canton and I was soon to discover that it was her maiden voyage and that she had a gross weight of 15,700 tons.

Madeleine and I went up the gangway while my Grandfather supervised the loading of my trunk into the ship's hold. When this had been done he joined us on board and we made our way to the Purser's office. I was introduced to the Purser and he showed us to the cabin on F deck (In the bowels of the ship) that I was to share with three others. I left my suitcase on a lower bunk and looked through the closed porthole, which was never opened because it was virtually on a level with the sea. When we returned to A deck, the Purser phoned through to the ship's padre who was going to keep an eye on me during the voyage. Although we were introduced I never again saw him during the voyage.

Grandfather's Armstrong Siddeley car

Soon the sounding of the ship's bell gave notice to all those who were not sailing, to leave the ship. I said my final farewells to my grandparents, thanked them for all they had done and waved as they returned to the dockside. The gangway was lowered and very slowly the Canton, now about to start her voyage to Yokohama, slipped her moorings and made her way downstream. It was the evening of the 7th October 1938. I continued to wave to my grandparents until they disappeared from sight in the swirling fog. It was the last time I was ever to see my Grandfather as he died some years later of cancer of the throat.

Although I had a strong feeling of elation it suddenly struck me that I was now alone, knew no-one on board ship and would not be seeing my parents for at least one month. I would need to make sure that I disembarked when we reached Penang, make my way to the E & O Hotel for the night and catch a plane to Bangkok the following morning. I would not have to worry about my trunk as it would follow a day or two later by train from Singapore.

Feeling at a loose end and very lonely I leaned over the side of the ship and watched the Thames slip by until it was too dark to see the

S.S.Canton

water, but for the occasional silvery movement of the ripples set off from the bow of the ship as she glided slowly downstream assisted by two tugs. Through gaps in the fog it was sometimes possible to make out the sillhouette of a building but, with little else to do, I decided to go to my cabin.

When I reached F deck, there was a lot of movement with cabin doors opening and closing, mostly men putting their things in lockers and generally preparing for the voyage. On reaching my cabin I found difficulty in getting in. There were three men all strangers to each other and to me. Two were thin and gaunt while the third was huge and looked like a weight lifter. "Ullo sonny," he said, " You'd betta' ave the top bunk as if I fell on ye you'd be flattened." and he picked me up and deposited me on the upper bunk. Head room was very limited, but it made the top bunk cosier. If I turned on my right side I could look through the porthole and watch the sea. Between the two lower bunks was a foldaway wash basin. Locker space was limited, but adequate as far as I was concerned. I lay propped on one elbow surveying the activities below and glad to be out of the way. Inwardly my emotions were all mixed up. I was looking forward to joining my parents and brother whom I had not seen for three years but at the same time, apprehensive of the journey ahead. I also missed my grandfather to whom I had been very attached.

When the other three had finished pushing clothes into lockers, slamming the cabin door umpteen times and had settled down, I decided to visit the lounge for 2nd class passengers and to have a general look around the ship. The lounge was very impressive with beautifully french-polished wood panelling around the bar where drinks were served. A steward asked me if there was anything I would like, so I ordered an orange juice, conscious of the fact that I had little in the way of money to spend during the voyage. There were few people in the lounge so I sat in one of the plush chairs to have my drink. I have never been good at sitting still for long so as soon as my glass was empty I got up to explore the ship. I soon discovered that second class passengers were not permitted to enter first class areas of the ship. There was a swimming pool that I would enjoy when the weather was warmer, and also play areas on deck where passengers could play quoits, badminton and other deck games. Having satisfied my curiousity, for the time being, I returned to my cabin, put on my pyjamas and climbed the ladder to my bunk. My three companions came in a little later and to my surprise they all slept in their underwear. That night as I lay watching the sea through the porthole I wondered if this was real, or whether it was all a dream and whether, on waking I would find that I was still at Fleet. Eventually I fell asleep to the pounding of the ship's engines.

I was awakened in the morning by a commotion in the cabin. The big man was washing at the basin but, although he turned off the tap, the water had not stopped and the water level in the basin was rising faster than it could drain away. Cursing, he gave a sudden twist, the water stopped flowing, but the tap broke off in his hand. This was not the only problem; when the cabin door was opened we discovered that F deck was awash with water. It was then that we learnt that there was a problem with the drainage, or lack of it, on F deck. The Canton had to berth at Southampton for a day so that the matter could be rectified and a new tap fitted to our basin.

There were no further problems until we reached the Bay of Biscay. Due to rough weather the ship rolled and lurched very badly and I was convinced that it would capsize . One minute we were in a trough with a wall of water 40 feet above us and the next moment we were on top of the wall about to be thrown off. I remained in the cabin while in the two lounges, chairs, tables and glasses and anything not properly secured was thrown from wall to wall. There were a number of injuries which required the attention of the ship's doctor. Sea water cascaded down the stairs whenever a wave broke over the ship. As the cabin became very stuffy, I went on deck when things became calmer, and sat on a bench where I was violently sick and felt very sorry for myself. The idea of food did not appeal. When the gong rang for lunch, two monks, dressed in brown cassocks with rope belts and leather sandals, seeing my distress, asked if they could help. I felt too ill to say anything but "Thank you," and shook my head from side to side. A few minutes later they re-appeared with two buttered bread rolls. It was with considerable trepidation that I bit into one of the rolls but, to my surprise, I enjoyed what I was eating and very soon had eaten both. One of the monks gave me a blessing and from then onwards I never again felt ill.

I and many other passengers were glad when we reached Gibraltar, where it was announced that A deck was top heavy.

Gibraltar to Aden

Gibraltar was our first port of call since we had left Southampton, and when we docked I decided to have a look around the Rock. At first I found it very peculiar walking on dry land as I still had my sea legs. I saw the Barbary Apes and had a look in some of the shop windows but, as we were to set sail within two hours, I made my way back to the ship. We docked next at Marseilles to pick up passengers and then went on to Malta where we took on more provisions before setting sail once again. Unfortunately, as the Canton left the harbour it got stuck on a mud bank for two hours and there she stayed until the tide rose sufficiently for her to float free. One day as we sailed through the Mediterranean I was asleep in a deck chair when a boy kicked away the support and I crashed to the deck, unhurt except for my pride. I got to my feet and went for the culprit. We fought until separated by two men. The boy's mother apologised to me as she witnessed what had happened. At Port Said we were entertained by "Gulli Gulli" men. They are swindlers of every conceivable description, pick pockets, cheats who will sell you anything at extortionate prices, but always very plausible. At first I simply watched their antics through the cabin porthole. Dilapidated buses occasionally drove along the dockside trying to get through the throng of people. When one of these buses was obliged to stop I actually watched a "Gulli Gulli" man deftly remove a wrist watch from someone whose arm was hanging out of the window. The owner of the arm was apparently quite unaware of what was going on as the arm never moved. I enjoyed Port Said. The ship had docked for some hours and being a small boy, I was not troubled by the pedlars. When ashore I never ventured far afield for fear of getting lost and missing the boat. There was no sign off the padre who was supposed to be keeping an eye on me and who I had not seen since we were introduced.

On leaving Port Said the Canton entered the Suez Canal and sailed straight into a sand storm. Doors and portholes had to be secured, but the sand seemed to get into everything. I was caught on deck at the time; the sand stung my face and hands to such an extent that I was forced to take shelter in the lounge where a kind gentleman gave me a glass of orange. The ship was obliged to anchor until the storm had passed. As we sailed through the Sweet Water Canal there was a full moon which created an eerie half light that allowed me to see the surrounding area, which consisted of vast tracks of sand. To the East the Sinai desert, to the West, Egypt. There was also the occasional dredger that slowly came into view like some pre-historic monster and which was there to keep the canal open to navigation. By early morning we passed Suez at the southern end of the canal and entered the Gulf of Suez and so on to the Red Sea. Here the water was beautifully clear and I found it fascinating to watch the multi-coloured fishes and marine life of every description. As we continued southward passing Port Sudan we entered the neck of the Red Sea and sailed due East to the next port of call, Aden. Here we docked for a full day taking on further provisions. I joined a bus ride around the town. I found very little of interest except for huge deposits of salt. Slightly inland from the sea there were a large number of what seemed to be manmade lakes, probably around 50 feet in diameter. In all probability they used to contain sea water which had dried out in the heat of the sun leaving behind a brilliant deposit of white translucent salt crystals.

A memorable birthday

I was leaning over the stern of the ship watching the wake as it trailed behind like a long string of pearls. Spray produced from the bow made rainbows as the sun shone through the droplets of water. On this her maiden voyage the Canton had left the salt lakes of Aden two days ago, the 23rd October, to cross the Indian Ocean and her next port of call was Bombay on the 27th October 1938. As I watched the sea, I noticed a shark, accompanied by a school of porpoises that were jumping out of the sea then falling back with a splash. They seemed to have a kind of rhythm all jumping and falling simultaneously giving the overall impression of a sea monster.

As I studied the water there were two things on my mind. After Bombay there would be only one further port of call, Colombo, and then on to Penang where I was to disembark, find the E.&.O Hotel then fly the following morning to Bangkok, where my parents and brother would be waiting to meet me.

Today, the 25th October, was my tenth birthday, which I had hoped to celebrate at home, but it was not to be. As my birthday always fell during term time it was never mentioned at school and by the time I had arrived at my grandparents' Bayswater flat, it was forgotten.

The steward was announcing that tea was now being served, by banging a gong as he walked around the decks. Usually I dashed to the dining room where tea was laid, but today I was deep in thought, eagerly contemplating the prospect of seeing my parents and younger brother in a few days' time. Coming out of my reverie I made my way to the dining room and was thunderstruck when the band broke into 'Happy birthday to you' and everyone got to their feet clapping. I paused looking around to see if anyone else had a birthday on the same day as me, when a steward came up and led me to a table in the centre of the room. On the table was an enormous cake in the shape of the Canton. It was covered in white icing with the name depicted either side of the bow in red with ten candles evenly spaced around the deck. It had been made for me by the catering staff. I was asked to cut the first slice and then a steward took over. The cake having finally been sliced into many pieces it was passed around to the passengers. When the stewards returned having served everyone there was none left for me. Inwardly, I was not disappointed as birthday cake has never been a favourite of mine, but I was touched by this kind gesture.

On the 27th October the Canton berthed at Bombay and I ventured ashore for a few hours. (I never suspected that five years later I would be back handing out cups of tea and food from a mobile canteen, to fire-fighters) I remember little of this short visit but I could not help smiling when I heard that the police in their blue uniforms and yellow berets were known affectionately as the Bombay Buttercups.

Having taken on further provisions, the Canton sailed the next day arriving at Colombo two days later. Again, I disembarked for only a short time, as we were to set sail almost immediately. I preferred Colombo to Bombay for although I only saw a small part of the town, it appeared to be most attractive and a lot quieter.

Chapter 3

Penang to Bangkok

On the 3rd November we arrived at Penang where I disembarked for the last time; it was eleven o'clock in the morning and very hot. The sun blazed down and a heat haze appeared to rise up from the ground, like a mirage. As I looked around, the buildings seemed to quiver and the bicycle rickshaws were zigzagging toward me; at least, that is the impression it gave. Clutching my small suitcase in my left hand I hailed a rickshaw and was immediately surrounded by a dozen or more. I chose the one that looked the cleanest. Ascending I said, "The E. & O Hotel, please." The journey only took ten minutes. I got out and said, "Please wait a minute while I get change for my English money in the hotel." "English money O.K." he replied. Producing a shilling from my purse his face lit up. I gave it to him, obviously I had paid too much. I thought to myself that the next time I wouldn't make the same mistake.

After I had booked in, the porter showed me to my room. It was magnificent, though I am told it is now somewhat rundown; furnished in oriental opulence with lattice blinds and open windows to let the humid air circulate. It was a large room. A double bed stood against one wall and above it there was a wooden frame supporting a mosquito net, which, when one pulled a cord lowered the net to the floor so that it surrounded the bed. On the bed was a beautiful silk counterpane decorated with dragons and embroidered in wonderful colours. On the opposite side of the room stood a double wardrobe, made from teak, probably Burmese judging by the ornate carvings. I had seen so much teak when previously in Bangkok that I recognised it immediately. My parents had similarly carved Burmese furniture at home, although not carved on such a grand scale. The centre of the wardrobe contained drawers, with hanging compartments on either side, one for ladies' clothes and the other for men's suits. As I only had a small suitcase and would be leaving early the next morning, there seemed little point in unpacking.

In the middle of the room a lacquer-topped table supported on bamboo legs and surrounded by four well-upholstered reclining chairs, also in bamboo. There was a bedside table on either side of the bed, highly carved, but not made of teak. This puzzled me as I could not remember ever having seen it before. About a month after returning home I mentioned the tables to my father who had been to the E. & O. Hotel. After thinking awhile he suggested that it was probably yamane clogwood which has a much finer grain and is carved in Burma for smaller, more decorative items.

Next to the door to the bathroom stood a chest of drawers. The dressing table had been placed in between the two very large windows and supported a triple mirror. A large fan hanging from the high ceiling and gently turning, kept the room pleasantly cool. The bathroom was more utilitarian with a plain enamelled caste-iron bath, a basin and toilet. I had seen hotels in Rangoon and Mandalay and although my memory of these is now very dim I am sure they did not compare with the sumptuousness of the E.& O.

After having a bath, as I was sticky due to the high humidity, I made my way to the dining room as I was famished. There were 16 dishes on the menu for lunch, consisting mainly of starters, like tropical fruits, small fish and salads. three main courses and a good selection of sweets. Looking at the waiter I asked, "I'm hungry, how many dishes am I allowed or do I have just one of each?" "You may have as many as you wish," said the waiter, who was dressed in white with a matching turban. I ordered a starter, and as the helping was small I went through all the starters one after the other. These were followed by one main course and I finished off with all the sweets, which like the starters, were not particularly substantial.

In the afternoon I strolled around Penang which, at the end of the eighteenth century, had been a penal settlement. Now it was a prosperous island with tree lined-roads and fine public buildings. I watched small native boats sailing majestically in and around the harbour. Nobody was in a hurry; even the bicycle rickshaws leisurely wove their way in and out of the traffic. Having little money, I did no shopping, but instead admired the multitude of goods on offer. The food shops sold a vast array of spices. One particular store was selling gentlemen's clothing, silk shirts and silk pyjamas were on display in the window; this made me quite envious as I have always liked the feel of silk next to the skin. Another shop sold ladies' handbags made from crocodile skins.

I returned to the hotel for tea with cucumber sandwiches and cakes, all very traditionally British. It was now five o'clock and I knew that before long the sun would be setting so I enquired at reception for details of what was worth a visit and was given a pamphlet of things to see and do. In the middle of the island is a mountain about 2500 feet, at the base of which is the Buddhist temple of Ayer Itam where I watched the monks in their saffron robes carrying their begging bowls, which reminded me of Bangkok. There are also beautiful gardens but, regrettably my time was short. After an early dinner I decided to go to bed as I was very tired and I would anyway have to be up early so as to get to the airport by 7 am the following day.

As it turned out I was so excited at the thought of seeing my parents and brother that I hardly slept. After a hurried breakfast, I packed my bag with a change of clothes and caught the bus to Bayan Lepas airport which is situated ten miles south of the capital George Town. I arrived early and checked in at at the airport well before the time of departure. An airport official from KNILM gave me a hand suitcase for the journey of which I was very proud and which, incidentally, is still in use. It is dark blue and has a metal plate beneath the handle printed on which are the letters KLM. The plane was a Dakota DC3 and painted on the nose was the name OEHOE (Dutch for Eagle Owl.) KNILM aeroplanes operating in the Far East were all named after owls and this particular aeroplane was to play an important part in my life some three years later. The Indonesians maintained that KNILM stood for *Kalau naik ini lekas mati* which loosely translated means, 'if you go in this you will soon be dead,' and what followed could have confirmed their fears.

We took off on time. There were only about seven passengers on board. In 1938 the pilots used to take the planes down low, literally skimming the treetops so that the passengers could see the wild animals running in all directions. I found this very interesting and could easily make out many different kinds, such as elephants, rhinocerous, tigers, leopards, deer, both large and small, and many more.

It was on just such a descent that I was in trouble. The aircraft was not pressurised and I got accute earache as the plane descended. A stewardess gave me boiled sweets and chewing gum, but I was in agony and screaming with the pain; my ears popped every time we altered height which also bothered me. When we gained height the pain left me and I once more took an interest in whatever was going on below.

We descended a second time and again I screamed from pain. By now we had crossed the Malay/Siam border and had been flying about an hour. The flat scrub land had been replaced by dense tropical rain forest of mainly teak and rubber, so the stewardess told me. Suddenly, the port engine started to splutter then stopped; black smoke poured from the engine. I and the other passengers immediately thought that the plane was on fire, but there were no flames to be seen. As the pilot could not get the engine started again he was faced with another problem. The stewardess entered the passenger compartment and said, " Because of the failure of one of the engines we cannot gain height, nor can we safely bank to return to a military airport in Malaya, as we are too close to the tree-tops. The chief pilot proposes to fly on in hope of landing safely on the sand banks of the Luang river, which is tidal. Meanwhile, please secure your seat belts and lean forward with your head tucked into your chests." Everyone did as they were told. The atmosphere was tense, not a word spoken. Unfortunately, when we reached the Luang it was high tide and there was no sand to be seen. While all this was going on I was still writhing in agony and was taking little interest in our future. We crossed the river and I noticed many rice fields which had been planted near the river and its tributaries. A few minutes later we were again over the rain forest when suddenly, the pilot saw an opening in the trees and dropped the plane. There was no time to lower the undercarriage or for anyone to utter a word, it all happened so fast. We hit the ground with a thud and as the plane careered along the grass it was possible to see the forest looming in front of us as we continued out of control. Luckily, we came to a halt about twenty feet from where the forest began once again. Apart from being very shaken and bruised no one was any the worse for the incident. My earache started to ease.

The pilot came to talk to us. The grassy stretch of land we were on had been cultivated by the local inhabitants; they were now all around the plane staring, mouths open in wide-eyed astonishment. "For your own safety, on no account is anyone permitted to leave the plane," said the pilot. "The natives are probably very friendly, but we cannot afford to take risks." The plane was on a slight tilt, with the tip of the port wing resting on the ground. The door furthest from the ground was opened to let in air. As it was still only about 8 am. the temperature had another few hours to go before reaching its zenith, so we were relatively cool. "All this time our radio operator has been in touch with a Siamese air force station," said the pilot, "and arrangements have been made for you all to be taken by truck, along with your baggage to the house of a local rubber planter; I am afraid it will be a bumpy ride, but we will get you there safely."

Two hours later a military truck appeared; our baggage was first taken from the plane and placed behind the driver's compartment. As I walked to the truck I looked behind and noticed the huge rut made on impact and the channel carved in the ground until the plane came to a standstill. Crops had been mowed down and in their place large and small fragments of metal lay scattered around. I felt sorry for the natives and hoped that someone would recompense them for the damage caused to their livelihood. It was a miracle that our pilot had managed to avoid the bamboo and mud huts that stood not far from where the plane struck the ground. I and the other passengers then climbed in and the tailgate was secured. Jungle roads, as far as they exist, are primitive and judging by the way we were thrown from side to side, it felt as though the road consisted of one pot hole joined to the next.

It took us about an hour to reach the house of the English rubber planter and his wife. They greeted us with open arms. It was obvious they had few visitors and were pleased to see us. We were looked after like royalty; a truly excellent lunch was served followed later in the afternoon by tea. While the grownups chatted together I wandered around the grounds, which were not very extensive and surrounded by jungle. Many of the trees produce latex from which rubber is manufactured. In particular I was fascinated by the animal life. Fire ants, flies, bees, wasps, mosquitos, flying beetles and beautifully coloured butterflies abounded. The rubber planter's wife, Patricia, came out to see me.

"Are you all right?" she asked.

"Yes, fine," I replied, "What are those small olive green birds with brightly coloured heads?"

"They are called bulbuls." She paused and then said, "Have you ever been to the East before?"

"Oh yes," I replied, "I am on my way to join my parents in Bangkok where I have lived for three years when I was younger. Can I ask you another question?"

"Of course," Patricia replied.

"I have noticed some flying animals in the trees which I have never seen before. Some look like lizards and some like squirrels, do you know what they are?"

"Yes, they're exactly as you've described them. Somehow the lizards are able to extend their bodies outwards when they jump from a tree and then glide down to a lower branch; they don't actually fly, in the true sense of the word, and the squirrels behave in the same way. It is interesting to watch them as they never miss their footing."

Patricia then went back to join her other guests indoors. The sun was beginning to set and the crackling sound of the grasshoppers was slowly being replaced by the sound of crickets. As darkness fell I listened to the noises of the jungle, the croaking of frogs, the screeching of monkeys, and many unrecognisable sounds. The jungle seemed to be alive with activity even in the dark. I went indoors.

The house faced on to a small river about 30 feet wide, probably the Luang or one of its tributaries. At 10 pm we all got into a launch which belonged to the rubber planter and started downstream to Ban Don which is on the railway line between Singapore and Bangkok. It was pitch black, there was no moon to be seen and the clouds overhead were laden with rain, but it did not fall. As I sat in the stern of the boat I could make out certain objects due to a fluorescence that flashed occasionally in the water. The ripple from the bow of the launch also helped me to discern nearby objects such as water lilies, reeds and the occasional water snake It was a slow twisting journey as the river meandered through the trees. Strange animals made even stranger noises from time to time as if to say "Beware, brethren, man is on the prowl," followed by scurrying feet away from the river bank. Left on my own I trailed a hand in the water picking up sticks or anything that might be of interest. A log appeared by the side of the boat and leaning out I put a hand on it so as to push it along. Suddenly, with a tremendous swish the log came to life. I had disturbed a crocodile. In panic I fell back into the boat and never again touched anything in the water.

I think it was around midnight when we reached Ban Don and the railway station, about 200 miles north of the Siam/Malay border.

The train duly arrived and we all clambered aboard. Most of the luggage was placed in the goods wagon but I held on to my KLM suitcase. Many of the compartments were full, but I eventually found a seat and was most pleasantly surprised to see three people whom I had met on the Canton. They had disembarked at Singapore and caught the train to Bangkok. Despite the early hours of the morning they were all curious to know what had happened. It took me a good half hour to tell them why the plane had to make an emergency landing and all that followed. By the time I had finished I was exhausted and I remember nothing more of the journey until late in the morning. Everyone in the compartment had considerately kept quiet knowing that I was worn out. The train drew into Bangkok early in the afternoon and there were my parents and brother to meet me. My father told me that they had waited at Bangkok airport from 10 am to 4.30 pm before news came through of the flight I was on the previous day.

Chapter 4

Bangkok

My parents lived in Mamoi, a large colonial style house opposite Lumpini Park. The house was separated from the park by Sathorn road and a klong. Because Bangkok is situated at sea level it has many water ways to help drain the land. Some klongs are big enough for boats to sail on, others just a small stream of almost stagnant water. The approach to our house was along a pebble drive with the house itself built on a slight rise to keep it dry during the monsoon. The large, teak front door at one end of the house was approached up a number of shallow stone steps. Opening the door I looked straight into the lounge, a large room, some thirty feet long by twenty feet wide with a wooden floor, covered here and there with small Chinese rugs, arranged in such a fashion so as to complement the positioning of the armchairs and settees. At the far end of the lounge were two, three foot buttresses, protruding from the outer walls between which were two, fourteen foot wide wooden stairs up into the dining room which was twenty feet square. The kitchen area which could not be seen as you enter the house, was approached through a door on the left side of the furthest wall. The whole was open plan. One of the most striking features was the large three-inch thick teak dining table, almost impossible to move it was so heavy. My parents employed a Chinese 'boy', (equivalent to an English butler) and this table was his pride and joy. Ah Fong, for that was his name, grew the nail on one of his little fingers until it was about an inch long and used it to remove any obstinate blemishes he found on the table top, which he regularly polished with loving care. The table was so highly polished that the sunlight from the open windows reflected off the surface casting shadows on the walls. At meal time a salt cellar was placed beside every glass and we were expected to put at least one spoon of salt into the glass of water every lunch time; because of the heat and humidity we all perspired copiously so it was essential to replace lost salt. It also helped to prevent cramp. Before going out, Mother usually left a daily menu

Mamoi, our house in Bangkok

for cook to have ready for each meal, but when she allowed cook a free hand we always ended up with caramel custard for dessert. In fact I had so many caramel custards that I now cannot stand the sight of them let alone eat one.

Shuttered windows on both side walls were kept open during the day to take advantage of any breeze that might occur. From the ceiling, in both lounge and dining room, hung a large rotating fan which could be regulated. In the corner of the lounge immediately left of the front door was a modern looking standard lamp that overhung a comfortable armchair and in which father sat to read his newspaper in the evening. Against the right buttress stood a glass-fronted teak bookshelf full of leather bound books, positioned here to be away from the sun's rays but supporting a table lamp. The books were all to do with the mathmatics of astronomy, one of my father's hobbies. Another, longer, bookshelf stood against the left wall with a larger lamp on top. To the right of the front door a flight of stairs disappeared to the floor above. All the walls were painted in a neutral stone colour, and all woodwork in a clear varnish. When evening drew in the geckos appeared, as if from nowhere, climbing up the walls and across the ceiling. Also known as towkays they are lizards, brown in colour, with adhesive toes which enables them to climb vertical shiny surfaces as well as running across the ceiling without falling off. From nose to the tip of their tail they can grow up to a foot long. I would take a sadistic delight in trying to hit them with a rubber band. If frightened they would drop their tails and run off, but a new tail soon grew again.

The lower part of Mamoi up to first floor level was built of brick to avoid destruction by termites, and the upper part of wood. Like the ground floor, the first floor was open plan. All upstair doors were similar to those seen in American western films that are open both top and bottom and swing backward and forward. Windows were slatted in the upstair rooms and in the very large verandah that went right across the front of the building and overhung part of the terrace below. There was a large bathroom and shower. Very occasionally I would find a snake cooling itself by lying in the enamel lined bath and once curled around a brass door handle. My parents slept in the room opposite the top of the stairs. The adjoining room was where Jon and I slept and, last of all the bathroom. I wore silk pyjamas at night but usually removed the jacket because I was so hot. In the cooler weather Jon and I had a single sheet we could pull up if needed. A mosquito net supported from the ceiling enveloped our beds and was tucked under the mattress. Nevertheless each morning when I awoke I invariably found mosquito bites on feet and hands where they had been touching the net. Fortunately, I never developed malaria so must assume that the mosquitos did not carry the disease.

From the upstair verandah we were able to see Sathorn road and the klong beyond, where sampans and other small boats sailed, drifted, or were rowed along. I often saw water rats and there was much debris thrown into the water so that it was anything but clean. The other side of the klong was Lumpini Park, with loudspeakers strapped to many of the trees. At festival time the latest popular songs blared out. The singers always sounded as though they had sore throats as the modulation was poor. One song that has always remained in my memory goes:

Sia-chai lamer
Sia-chai
Sia laeu
Sia pai
Hami dee kwah
Sia-chai lamer, Sia-chai

The garden was extensive both back and front and around the perimeter of the grounds was another klong, a small one, about three to four feet wide. We tended to avoid the water as it was the home of many snakes, mainly the banded krait which is highly poisonous. However snakes are usually harmless unless you upset them. We also had Sally, a scotty dog, who dealt very effectively with the snakes.

On the terrace, beneath the upstair verandah, a ping-pong table leant against the main wall when not in use. One day Jon and I decided to have a game of table tennis, but as caution was always the main priority I first looked behind the table and there sure enough was a banded krait curled up asleep. Picking up Sally I pushed her between wall and table saying "Snakes, Sally get it." Sally dutifully went behind the table, sniffed the snake, trod all over it and reappeared the other end wagging her tail. The snake hardly moved. On my third attempt, Sally got the message. Grabbing the snake by the head she pulled it from behind the table, then all hell was let loose. The banded krait which was about eight feet long reared up with Sally hanging on for dear life; it then brought Sally down on the concrete terrace with a dreadful thud. Sally hung on undaunted. The fight continued for a good three minutes, the snake gradually getting slower. The struggle over, the snake lay dead, and Sally, who seemed none the worse for her ordeal was again wagging her tail as if to say, "Are there any more you wish me to take care of?" Apart from Sally we could always rely on Sammy to deal with the snakes.

Sammy

Sammy was an uninvited guest, but a very welcome one. From the tip of his nose to the end of his bushy tail Sammy was about twenty-one inches in length. He was sleek but perhaps a little plump, probably because Cook would put out a plate of leftovers for him to eat every day. Sammy instinctively knew when Cook had put out his daily meal by the back door of the house and rushed up the garden, ate it in a flash and rushed back to the klong that surrounded the garden. His speed was electrifying and he was the scourge of the snakes that lived in the klong.

Like most animals Sammy knew who were his friends. Occasionally, but only occasionally, Sammy would come to see Jon and me as we played in the garden. He allowed us to stroke him ever so gently, but never to pick him up. When stroked he would shake himself violently and we would be covered in a fine spray as Sammy was permenently wet.

Sammy's fur was brownish-grey in colour, his two forelegs considerably shorter than the back legs. Sammy would rush about in the garden, suddenly stop, and sit upright on his back legs balanced with the aid of his bushy tail and survey the garden, to see what was going on. In this position he would look like a very large sleek squirrel with much more hair and thicker tail. He had a pointed nose which twitched when on the alert and if he was disturbed by an enemy, his hair would bristle like a dog when at bay. His small feet ended in sharp, very sharp nails. He had beady eyes and his teeth were like razor blades. Sammy had no fear; watching him attack a cobra or banded krait six to eight feet long was an experience. The snakes never stood a chance. Sammy would rush the snake which would strike. With incredible speed Sammy would sidestep the fangs as the snake struck , turn, and bury his teeth just behind the snake's head. If not killed instantly the snake would rear up to shake off his opponent but one thing Sammy never did was to let go. Sammy was also very good at disposing of snakes' eggs and rats.

I never discovered if there was a Mrs. Sammy and never saw any baby Sammys. I never found where he lived but often had the feeling I was being watched as I searched for clues about the garden. What happened to Sammy when my parents and Jon were interned by the Japanese I shall never know, but I often think of those happy days with Sammy. If you have not already guessed, Sammy was a mongoose and Jon and I, in fact, called him Rikki-Tikki-Tavi after Rudyard Kipling's 'The Jungle Book', but that would have given the game away.

Having already spent three years in Siam from the age of three to six I soon became familiar with the daily routine. My father was responsible for the financial side of the Bombay Burma Trading Corporation in Bangkok. Apart from taking care of the accounts, he was jointly responsible, with the Mill Manager, Mr. A.J.Williams, our next door neighbour on Sathorn Road, for two small cargo ships that plied between Bangkok and Singapore, carrying teak. During the day my mother, brother and I spent much time at the Royal Bangkok Sports Club, swimming, so as to keep cool. The sports club was a long, low, sprawling building, in the front a large swimming pool, at the side two squash courts and a number of tennis courts

Royal Bangkok Sports Club

and, to the rear an 18 hole golf course which was transversed by klongs to such an extent that golfing enthusiasts were obliged to use floating golf balls. Beyond the golf course, though not often used, was a race course with stables for the horses.

At times I was left to my own devices and would go and see Ah Fong. Before joining my parents he had worked for a French family and also a family from Czechoslavakia and had picked up a smattering of both languages. Ah Fong taught me how to play Mah Jong the way it is played in China and we made up a foursome with the coolie and cook who were also Chinese. At first I was terribly slow and it seemed always to be my turn to make a move, but eventually I mastered the game and soon became proficient which was to be of great benefit to me when I got to India.

My father was a strict disciplinarian and I was expected to do what I was told. He was always fair, but when I was really naughty he would remove the leather belt around his waist, put me between his legs so that I couldn't move, and thrash me with the belt.

The snake farm

Bangkok boasts a snake farm, known as The Queen Saovabha Memorial Institute. I believe that at the time there were only two in the world, the other being in Brazil, so I was told. Alternate Wednesdays was the day for extracting venom from the snakes and it used to interest me to watch how it was done. Dominating the scene was a large oval concrete pit divided into three partitions and surrounded by a wall about three feet high on the outside, the base of the pit about eight feet from the top of the wall. It housed king cobras, cobras and banded kraits each in their own partition. Around the inside perimeter was a three foot-wide channel full of water. On the base of the pit were many semicircular, domed houses for the snakes. They looked like a huge ball cut in half with four openings so that the snakes could come and go. These houses were made of concrete but could be lifted quite easily by means of metal handles positioned around each dome. The snakes were to be found either in a domed house or in the water during the heat of the day. Many frogs also jumped around in the pit, put there for the snakes to feed on.

When home from school I frequently visited the snake farm which I found quite fascinating. At 10 o'clock every other Wednesday morning a Siamese doctor and his assistant placed a short ladder into the pit and then climbed down. While the doctor put his equipment on the ground his assistant would remove a domed house beneath which was a tangle of snakes. Picking one out, apparently at random, he would grip the snake behind the jaw and press hard forcing open the mouth while his other hand held the writhing body. The doctor would suck milk from a bottle using a glass tube and having sufficient milk put a finger over the end that was in his mouth so that the milk would not run out. The open end of the tube was then thrust into the mouth and down the throat of the snake. He then blew down the tube dispensing the milk inside the snake. This having been accomplished he picked up a microscope slide which must have had a covering of some kind of latex. The slide was placed sideways into the jaws of the snake and

Domed houses at the snake farm, Bangkok

the assistant then slowly released the head. The snake bit hard on the glass releasing the venom. The doctor having retrieved his slide, his assistant would cast the snake into the water. This process was repeated with just a few snakes from each section of the pit. I watched this bi-weekly procedure with mounting excitement wondering what would happen if something went wrong and the doctor or his assistant were bitten by a snake. I was soon to find out.

Inevitably there were occasions when Wednesday morning brought a larger than usual gathering of sightseers. I remember one day in particular when the assistant was in the pit of the king cobras along with the doctor when he, the assistant, decided to put on a show. He selected a snake and proceeded to provoke it. The king cobra reared up, head flattened, swaying from side to side, the snake hissing loudly with not a sound from any of the onlookers, its forked tongue shooting in and out like the piston of an express train at speed. By now the assistant and snake were about two feet apart with heads level; the snake was about eight to ten feet long. The assistant stood stock still seemingly hypnotising the snake, which did not strike. Suddenly a bird flew nearby distracting the assistant for a split second, but it was enough; the snake struck and the assistant reeled backwards and collapsed on the ground. The doctor, who like the rest of us was just a bystander watching the event, calmly took a syringe from his bag along with the antidote, filled the syringe and injected his assistant whom he then helped out of the pit. They were both back as usual a fortnight later.

I saw many other snakes, but the most frightening were the boa constrictor and the python. On the whole snakes are lazy animals. Having eaten they go to sleep until the next meal. In captivity the boa constrictor and python were housed in separate enclosures of heavy wire netting. On Wednesdays they were fed with a small live deer. The boa constrictor would wrap itself around the deer and swallow it whole which was a slow process and the deer could be seen moving inside the snake until finally crushed to death. The python on the other hand would wrap its coils around the deer, crush it to death and then swallow it. I paid many visits to the snake farm.

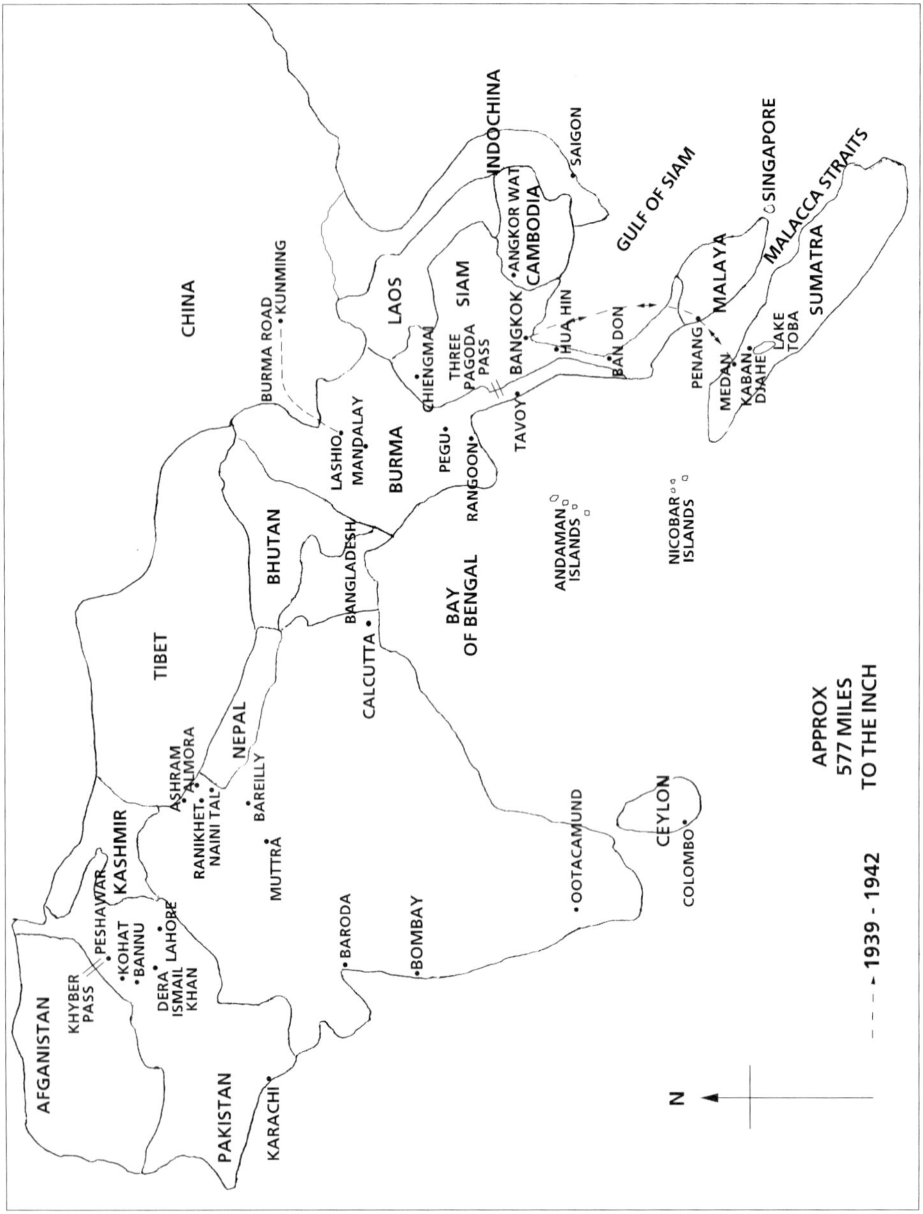

CHINA
BURMA ROAD
KUNMING
INDOCHINA
SAIGON
LAOS
SIAM
ANGKOR WAT
CAMBODIA
GULF OF SIAM
SINGAPORE
MALACCA STRAITS
SUMATRA
MALAYA
LAKE TOBA
PENANG
MEDAN
KABAN DJAHE
BAN DON
HUA HIN
BANGKOK
THREE PAGODA PASS
CHIENGMAI
TAVOY
PEGU
RANGOON
BURMA
MANDALAY
LASHIO
BHUTAN
BANGLADESH
CALCUTTA
BAY OF BENGAL
ANDAMAN ISLANDS
NICOBAR ISLANDS
TIBET
NEPAL
ALMORA
ASHRAM
RANIKHET
NAINI TAL
BAREILLY
MUTTRA
KASHMIR
PESHAWAR
KOHAT
BANNU
LAHORE
DERA ISMAIL KHAN
KHYBER PASS
AFGANISTAN
PAKISTAN
KARACHI
BARODA
BOMBAY
OOTACAMUND
CEYLON
COLOMBO
APPROX 577 MILES TO THE INCH
1939 - 1942
N

Chapter 5

Sumatra

I enjoyed being home, but inevitably I began counting the days that I must once again go to school. I was now ten years old and it was after Christmas and the New Year that my father took me aside and explained that he and my mother had decided to send me to Highlands School, Kaban Djahe, Sumatra. It was a co-educational school 800 or so miles from Bangkok. There were to be two terms each year. (This was because of the distance most of the pupils had to travel), with a holiday in the summer and one in the winter, so I would be flying to and from school four times every year.

In fact my parents had little choice of school unless I was sent to Australia, at five times the distance, and vastly greater expense. Mr. Cookson, the headmaster of Highlands School and his wife, organised the school on the lines of an English public school. The only other British school in the general area of Bangkok was a girls' convent school in the Cameron Highlands of Malaysia. It was here that our best friends and next-door neighbours were to send their daughter, Fay Williams. Fay was a year older than I.

So on the 17th January 1939 I said a very tearful goodbye to my parents and boarded the train for the short journey to the airport. My mother had given me a bar of chocolate which I unwrapped, but being so upset, I threw the chocolate out of the window and put the wrapping paper in my mouth. On arriving at the airport there was no difficulty in finding the plane as only one was to be seen. I climbed the steps into the KNILM Dakota DC3 along with other passengers and we took off. We were to land at Penang before flying on to Medan, the capital of Sumatra and the journey would take about five hours in all.

After half an hour's flying the co-pilot came into the cabin and said, "Would any passenger like to fly the plane under supervision?" Nobody stirred and most looked out of the windows as though nothing had been said. I tentatively put up my hand and thought I heard a groan from a number of the passengers. I was ushered into the cockpit and sat down next to the pilot who proceeded to demonstrate how the plane would react when moving the joy stick. I was told to take over. Gingerly, I moved the joy stick one way then the other and the plane banked one way then the other. I was having a fine old time when the stewardess appeared and said, "Please keep the plane on an even keel as two of the passengers are being sick." After 15 minutes I returned to my seat with glares from some of my fellow travellers. During the times I was invited into the cockpit over the next three years I got to know the pilots and radio operators very well and for me it was a wonderful experience.

We landed at Penang airport which in those days, I am told, was quite difficult, due to the surrounding hills. We all got out and made our way to the lounge for refreshments. As I was on my own, the pilots, who were Dutch, asked me to go with them to the staff area where they gave me biscuits and a drink. In time I was to become their unofficial mascot when I journeyed between the two capitals and was always invited to take refreshments with the pilots when we landed.

The distance from Penang to Medan as the crow flies is not far, about 170 miles over the Strait of Malacca; and so I arrived at Medan.

Bus ride to Kaban Djahe

This may be a good time for a brief review of my development. My early life was spent with my parents, then for three years, from seven to ten, I did not see them at all. A journey by ship from London to Penang followed by a flight and train to Bangkok taught me that I could stand on my own feet when travelling. The three years away from my parents were not happy ones. Now, barely two and a half months after joining them in Siam, I was off again into the unknown. My parents had never been to Sumatra so could give me no idea of what I could expect. My father had taught me that only babies and girls cry, but boys were expected to be brave. This meant that I began subconsciously to hide my feelings rather than share any emotion, for fear of being hurt in other ways. Subsequent events and disappointments in life have ensured that whatever emotion I show is merely superficial, a disguise for my real feelings.

So here I was in Sumatra, one of the largest islands in the world and divided in half by the equator. It was up to me to find my way to

Kaban Djahe, which was not difficult, as I simply took a rickety bus into the centre of town and with a little help found the right bus for school. Medan is on the East coast and Kaban Djahe in the mountain range that runs centrally down the whole length of the country. I boarded another rickety bus and we set off. Once clear of Medan the road started to climb and the bus started to groan, but somehow it managed to stagger upwards. Before long we came to the first of a whole series of hairpin bends which the bus could not negotiate without reversing, going forward, reversing again and so on about six times to get around one corner. This manoeuvre was literally hair-raising. At the apex of every corner a ramp had been constructed made of planks of wood and in turn these planks were supported by a number of rather flimsy-looking wooden poles driven into the hillside. The bus driver would negotiate the corner as far as possible, then reverse on to the ramp. Looking out of the window all I could see was a sheer drop of twenty to forty feet on to the tops of trees below. Traffic in the other direction caused further consternation with shouting and arm waving. At this point the monkeys joined in, swinging from tree to tree directly over our heads and chattering away and screeching at the top of their voices. The effect was pandemonium.

There were other distractions in the form of an occasional bus or lorry that had gone over the edge and rolled down the bank until halted by trees. However, nobody took any notice which left me with the belief that this was quite usual. And so we climbed up and up until we reached Brastagi 4800 feet above sea level and where the road levelled off. At Brastagi the bus stopped for a short break and everyone got out. I found little that interested me except for an extraordinary form of amusement which seemed to me to be so out of place in an otherwise rather mundane town. It consisted of a vibrating path with handrails on either side which shook backwards and forwards at considerable speed. The path led nowhere and there was no other form of entertainment anywhere to be seen and so appeared to be pointless.

We all returned to the bus and were soon at Kaban Djahe, the journey having taken a little over two hours not including the stop at Brastagi. The bus driver stopped near the school entrance and there waiting for me were a small group of people consisting of the Headmaster, his wife and a few boys. The Headmaster told Hank, an American, to take me to the dormitory I was to share with eleven other boys. En route Hank said, "Do you know what f— means?"

" No." I replied, so that by the time I arrived at the dormitory I had been fully apprised of the facts of life.

My luggage, consisting of a very large trunk and a tuck box made of teak and very heavy, preceded me by rail and sea, and had been placed by my bed. Mrs Cookson very soon appeared and removed all the clothing and put it away somewhere unknown to me. The empty trunk was then removed, leaving me with the tuck box. Once Mrs. Cookson had left I was joined by a large group of boys. "What food have you got?" asked a voice. As I had no idea what my mother had packed I opened the box and all the food disappeared as if by magic. I was to learn the hard way.

By the time I had settled in it was getting late in the afternoon so I was taken by some of the boys on a conducted tour of the extensive grounds. The boys' and girls' dormitories were well separated and in between was a very large building known as the 'Hall' which consisted of a huge room with windows all round and a wooden floor. To all intents it served as meeting room, games room , and sometimes as a lecture hall and examination room. There was also a junior school where the younger pupils were cared for by a matron. I cannot remember where the classrooms were in relation to the other buildings. The far side of the grounds was where Mr. and Mrs. Cookson lived with their three daughters, Nancy, Mary and Susan. All buildings were at ground level as Sumatra is subject to earthquakes. The playing fields were extensive and the whole compound was surrounded by a very thick hedge. In fact it was so thick that a number of boys, including me, managed to hollow out a secret hiding place in the hedge where we could hide and eat our ill-gotten gains, of which more, later.

As our group wandered slowly around the school grounds, we talked about our homes, families, what we enjoyed doing most, the do's and don'ts of school discipline, what the headmaster and his wife were like, what the teachers were like and a host of other things. During our wanderings I noticed that the sun was setting earlier than it did in Bangkok, as the school was only three degrees north of the equator and on a level with Kuala Lumpur in Malaysia.

Kaban Djahe

Kaban Djahe is situated between two active volcanoes, Mount Sibayak, which just smokes most of the time, and Mount Sinabung which is a boiling cauldron of lava. The clouds above the volcanoes were a beautiful orange colour, which mirrored the boiling lava below. The first time I saw this spectacle there was hardly a cloud to be seen but, when the monsoon arrived, the whole sky resembled a vast firework display. Fortunately for Kaban Djahe the eruptions of Mount Sinabung were not serious; only occasionally was a large boulder, about the size of a grand piano, thrown out of the mouth of the volcano and it would simply roll down the side glowing red and sending sparks in every direction.

   Sometimes on a weekend, and when practical, a master and a few of the pupils climbed up one side of the volcano and peered into the crater. The boiling lava, like some huge writhing yellow and orange animal was quite incredible to watch. As we stood staring, I, and most of the others must have realised how helpless man is compared with this demostration of the beauty and force of nature. The rim of the crater was six to ten feet wide where we stood but of course varied considerably from place to place. The ground was very friable being made of pumice and our feet would sink in up to the ankles. All the time spent at the mouth of the crater we had to be on the alert in case the wind changed. The sulphurous gases emitted from the volcano could suddenly envelop any unsuspecting person to the extent that it was impossible to see your feet and breathing became very difficult. On these occasions it was imperative to stay still until the wind blew the gases away and it was possible to see again. One false move could be fatal. I can only remember being caught in this way on one occasion and it was momentary; apart from the obvious danger, the fumes were most unpleasant and, as an asthmatic, I could hardly breathe and had to be helped down the volcano.

   I remember very little of Kaban Djahe as a town, but it must have been the size of a small country town in Britain. Virtually all the inhabitants worked on the plantations of tobacco, tea, corn, rubber, sisal and to a lesser extent pineapple. There were also spices like chillis both red and green, pepper, cloves, nutmeg, betel nut, and cinnamon which grew wild. In fact when our scout troop were out camping we would cut the bark from cinnamon trees and eat it. The plantations were owned and run by the Dutch. The high quality tobacco was much in demand in the USA as it is used for the outer wrapping of the best cigars.

Apart from volcanoes there is another geological feature that affects Sumatra. Earthquakes occur from time to time. Usually there were minor tremors; the ground would shake slightly and it was all over in seconds, but I do remember one occasion when it was more than just a tremor. At the time I was in a room of my own. When I had a bad asthma attack I was looked after by matron in the junior school. At night time I would sit up in bed inhaling Potters Patent Asthma Cure which used to smoulder away in the lid of a Wills Gold Flake cigarette tin. The smoke was supposed to relieve the asthma, but was a dismal failure. Perhaps I should have tried eating the liver of a fruit bat, as the natives do, to cure their asthma, but this idea was never encouraged. My wheezing and the smell of the asthma cure, only succeeded in keeping awake everyone in the dormitory. So I was moved to a room of my own. It was bare except for a bed , a bedside table on either side and a free-standing clothes cupboard about six feet high. On one table stood a glass and jug full of water and on the other my so called medications. The cupboard stood near the door and clear of the bed. It was night time and very dark, I was sitting up in bed and wheezing, desperately trying to exhale when the building started to shake violently. The cupboard toppled over and crashed to the floor and shattered. The quake lasted for about thirty seconds and was followed by minor tremors. Lights were switched on, matron and other members of the staff came rushing into the building to see if all was well. Thankfully, the only casualty was my cupboard but a curious thing had happened. The jug of water by my bedside had somehow moved from one bedside table to the other. There was no spilt water to be seen, the Potters Asthma Cure was unmoved and the glass remained on the table that the jug had been on. It was as though some supernatural element had moved the jug.

Because of asthma I rarely was able to lie flat in bed, instead I had to sit up all night and consequently I seldom ever slept for more than four hours at a time. Even now I only require four hours good sleep in 24 hours.

Another natural phenomenon which I have seen only once, was when a group of us were practising for a scout badge which involved tracking. At the time we were high up on a ridge of a hill when, looking westward we noticed a tornado which was working its way northward along the coast. It was an incredible sight. In the whirling, twisting, ever-changing spiral of air, with the apex somewhere on the ground, not visible to us but within the rising column, I could clearly make out small trees and all sorts of debris being drawn upwards, only to fall back to earth and be replaced with still more debris. So it worked its way slowly northward until lost from our sight.

Chapter 6

Highlands School

I was now ten and so far as my academic record went, I was probably average, except in mathematics and geography in which I usually came top of the class. On the other hand my ability in languages has always been hopeless unless I was living in a foreign country and was more or less obliged to converse in the native tongue. In Latin and English I could not get along with either grammar or literature, through lack of interest. My belief, that how a subject is taught is of paramount importance, held true when I eventually returned to school in England at the age of sixteen; I quickly went from bottom to the top three of the class in English Literature because it was so well taught by Mr. White, at Highgate School in London, who had the ability of making the subject most interesting. My parents wanted me to learn the piano, which was a disaster. The piano teacher was a very large lady and we shared a bench in front of the piano. Unfortunately, she occupied nine tenths of the bench and I kept on falling off the end every time she moved. This lasted for only three weeks and I sighed with relief.

One of my favourite subjects at school was carpentry. A large, rather scruffy-looking shed was used for this purpose, and was filled with benches and tools of every description. A fine array of saws from small to very large, hung from rusty nails along one wall. The beams supporting the roof were covered in cobwebs where spiders went about their daily activities of catching flies, or any other misguided insect that became ensnared in the webs. While they waited for a master to arrive, the boys would watch, with morbid curiosity, the activities of the praying mantises which were to be found on almost all window panes. Flies were always anxious to get to the sunnier parts of the shed and so would inevitably alight on a window pane for their appointment with death. As they turned this way and that trying to get through the glass, the flies would at some point face the praying mantis and would be hypnotised. Once this happened the fly moved slowly but surely toward its predator, seemingly unable to do anything else. The praying mantis would remain immovable until the fly was in reach, then suddenly, the two forelegs would shoot forward and grab the fly between head and thorax. Struggle as it might, and with rapidly vibrating wings, the fly would be eaten until only the wings remained, which gently spiralled down to the floor to become dust within a few days.

There was an unfortunate occasion when a group of boys were running to the carpentry lesson. All of us were carrying pieces of wood of varying shapes and sizes. Tom, a big lad, caught his foot in some wire lying on the ground and fell forward, putting his arm through one of the shed windows. On withdrawing the arm he caught it on the broken glass and cut himself very badly. I was right behind him and saw the damage before the blood started pouring out in every direction. A large triangular piece of flesh had been levered upwards and he had many other lacerations. Nothing ever seemed to worry Tom; he simply pushed the flap back into place and taking a dirty handkerchief from his pocket started to tie it around the injured arm. Fortunately, Mrs. Cookson witnessed what had occurred and proceeded to give first aid. When she had tied up the wounds she told me to take Tom straight to hospital. It was a 15 minute walk. On arrival we were ushered into the operating theatre where a doctor told Tom to sit on a stool while the nurse asked me to hold him steady while she prepared an injection. Tom never flinched and watched the proceedings, initially with interest, and then with what appeared to be utter boredom as he gazed around the room. Once the local anaesthetic had numbed the arm, the stitching started. The sight of the blood and the bright lights were all too much for me and I passed out. Tom had 29 stitches put in the arm but he went on as usual, as though nothing had happened.

Every week all the pupils wrote home. At first my letters were pitiful as I was so unhappy. Then my father wrote to the headmaster and thereafter my letters were censored by a member of staff so I could no longer express my feelings. Censoring ceased once I had stopped complaining and instead my father would return my letters corrected in red ink.

Games were my only forte during my school days but in Sumatra my activities were curtailed by asthma, which meant I was always goalkeeper when not laid up. At times the asthma became so bad that I would be taken to the hospital and given injections of adrenaline which gave me only temporary relief. When in this state I looked forward to the injections and to feeling my heart race, and to breathing properly, if only for one to two hours. I have often wondered if my parents realised how chronically I suffered from asthma in Sumatra as I never had an attack in Siam.

One of my favorite activities was roller skating in the 'Hall.' I became adept at this and usually joined the end of the snake pulled around in a circle by a group without skates. This meant I was travelling at an enormous speed holding the hand of the person next to me. There was one occasion when I was going so fast that I failed to hang on and went straight through an open window, landing on soft turf outside, without injury.

Once I had a heated argument with a boy by the name of Towkes Gross and we decided to box to see who was right. Towkes was considerably smaller than I but nevertheless gave me a hiding. I also took on the school champion as a bet that I could last three rounds without being knocked out. I won the bet by keeping well out of harm's way.

Hockey was the main team game played at Highlands School. The games' master was Swiss and very keen. To a large extent, the official rules of the game were not adhered to, which resulted in the master landing up in hospital with stitches in an eyebrow. As usual I was in goal.

Another activity was horse riding. I had never been on a horse, but was persuaded to mount the only docile horse in the stables. With help and advice from other boys we walked the horses, then went into a trot which was most uncomfortable, then cantered and finally galloped which was exhilarating. On our return journey to the stables I got a sudden severe pain in my back; I somehow managed to stop the horse and the pain went. Believing that I would be all right, I kicked the horse and off we went again. The pain immediately returned and I was unable to sit upright; there was no strength in my back and I fell off. Unfortunately, I could not extricate one of my feet from the stirrup so was dragged along the ground for about 100 yards. When I regained consciousness I was in hospital suffering from concussion.

A nurse said, "How do you feel?"

"I've got a nasty headache." I replied.

"Well that's not surprising after your fall, you've been in here for three hours, do you feel like a cup of tea?" said nurse.

"No thank you, when can I go back to school?"

"When doctor has seen you and only if he says you can return," replied nurse.

Half an hour later the doctor came in to examine me. "Well, you seem to have recovered and nurse tells me you wish to return to school which you can but, no games for a week and take it steady, don't rush around and come and see me in three days' time unless you feel ill or still have a headache tomorrow, in which case return to hospital immediately," said doctor.

"Thank you," I replied, rapidly getting dressed.

Rushing to the door nurse stopped me. "Doctor said take it steady, don't rush, walk back to school," said nurse. I did.

On the outskirts of Kaban Djahe and not far from the school, was a leper colony which was out of bounds for all pupils. We never entered the leper colony and I believe that the poor sufferers were taken care of by dedicated nuns who would eventually contract the disease and die many years later. The inmates of the colony were allowed to visit the town and to buy whatever they needed. They were always recognisable, clothed in an all enveloping tattered dark grey cloak of what looked like a coarse material. Around their necks hung a cow bell so that it rang as they moved to warn people away. The only parts of the body that were visible were the face, hands, and feet sometimes shod in sandals. As the disease attacks the extremities of the body first, I assumed that those who ventured from the colony must have been relatively new sufferers. Their fingers and toes were being eaten away and an occasional sore could be seen on the face. As the disease continued to destroy the body, sufferers would be bed- ridden until the day when the corpse would be burnt on a pyre. This whole horrible process would take around seven years, with no remission. We at the school were largely protected from the realities of life. The native population of northern Sumatra and in the region of Aceh were used to suffering; they were born to it and whatever might happen they took in their stride. Life was cheap.

It must be remembered that during the 19th and in the beginning of the 20th century the natives of Aceh were very fierce and practised cannabalism and headhunting. It was early in the 20th century that the Dutch had great problems when trying to pacify this area of northern Sumatra and it is believed that as many as 250,000 people lost their lives in the fighting. They were never completely subjugated and are still a proud and independent people.

At weekends we were allowed out of the school grounds and so often went into the town where we would see the lepers usually buying fruit. There was plenty of choice but coconut and bananas appeared to be the favourite. Vegetables were usually displayed on stalls outside the shop. Apart from food, traditional Batak native clothing, which is very colourful, could be bought, but the only shops of interest to the boys were those that sold sweets and other confections. Until one of the boys was caught, I am ashamed to say a group of us would go to a sweet shop and whilst one boy kept the owner in conversation the others helped themselves to a handful of sweets.

We had to adopt different methods if we wanted a pineapple, corn on the cob or sugar cane, as native guards kept an eye on the plantations. On these occasions, a boy who could run fast caused a distraction and inevitably the guards would rush to the spot where he was. Meanwhile, the other boys would help themselves to whatever they wanted and they took this back to school where it was hidden in the thick hedge where we had our hideout. After lessons had finished for the day we returned to the hedge to enjoy our ill-gotten gains. Sometimes we had a midnight feast, but this was a risky business as we were likely to be caught.

The dining room at Highlands School was large; we ate off trestle tables with long benches on either side. Down the centre of each table, spaced at regular intervals, were a series of small dishes each containing green chilli peppers to which we could help ourselves if we felt like it. On my first day at school I took a liberal helping of green peppers, believing them to be beans. With other boys watching with interest I took a mouthful then writhed in pain as I tried to cool my burning mouth with water, while the boys had a good laugh at my expense. I was not the first nor the last to learn the hard way about green peppers. After the main course, bowls of red rice, steaming hot, were placed on every table the idea being that if anyone was still hungry they should help themselves to the rice. Together with lots of gravy, the rice was delicious. The rice served at school was grown in Sumatra and when the husks were removed the grain was a pinky-red, and we were told, very nutritious, unlike polished rice. In Bangkok we ate purple rice and in Malaya black rice is available.

The best meal we had was the day before the end of term. In the school grounds there was a parallel line of huge trees. I have no idea what kind of trees they were but, bearing in mind that on average there was in excess of 300 inches of rain every year, in such tropical conditions they grew to enormous proportions. So on the last full day of term the trestle tables were set out in a line between the trees and on them placed dishes of rice tafel. This consists of a bed of rice with a host of side dishes of every description: nuts, mango, mangosteen, coconut, papaya, pumelo, avocado, fried banana, beans, chillis, egg plant, in fact just about everything you can think of and it was absolutely delicious.

The boys at Highlands School were no different from boys the world over and got up to pranks on numerous occasions. Some were highly dangerous. The games master visited the dormitories at night to see that all was as it should be. One night, in anticipation of his visit, we placed a fire bucket full of water balanced on top of the half open dormitory door. We had expected him to get soaked. Unfortunately, when he pushed open the door the bucket crashed down on his arm and broke it. Only his feet got wet. On yet another occasion we tied rope about a foot high from bed to bed across the floor separating the two sides of the room. In the dark the master failed to see the rope, tripped heavily and crashed to the floor, ending up with a bloody nose. These escapades did not go unpunished.

Midnight feasts were always popular. Food was either taken from the dining room or stolen from the village. We were caught red-handed when one of the boys brought in a durian. This is a large oval fruit with a prickly skin; the taste is delicious but the smell is appalling and it can only be eaten if you hold your nose. On this particular night Mr. Cookson, the headmaster, was somewhere in the school grounds and was assailed by the odour, so came to investigate. The whole dormitory was kept in at play time for the next three days, writing out lines as punishment. Lines were a favourite form of punishment and on a few occasions I had to write out 1000 lines for misbehaving. Another punishment was to stay in school while the scouts went on a camping weekend. We all loved camping and would have much preferred to write out lines but we never had a choice. I never heard of any boy being caned so I assumed that Mr. Cookson did not believe in corporal punishment.

Before the end of term we were deloused. This meant that each boy showered, washed and shampooed with a foul-smelling liquid which was intended to kill lice. I suspect it was a cautionary measure as we seldom became infected. On the other hand intestinal worms were quite common and if a boy reported with an irritating anus he would be given a large chocolate-coloured tablet about one inch in diameter that he chewed. It tasted of chocolate and was most pleasant; it also produced the desired results.

Top – *Boy Scouts India*
Below – *Badges I wore on my jacket in Bangkok*
Bottom right – *NEDERLAND ZAL HERRIJZEN (Netherlands shall rise again)*

Chapter 7

Scouts

During the three years I was at Highlands School there was a very active scout troup. I fear that I was one of the least active. All senior boys were members of the troop, and many very quickly became King Scouts. Three of the boys managed to obtain most, if not all, the badges in the scouting manual. On special occasions the badges were displayed on a wide band of material that went over the right shoulder, across the chest and up the back. After three years I had managed to become a King Scout and held badges for first aid, interpreter, tailor, pathfinder and various others. I was the most junior in the Wolf Patrol, being twelfth man as I had the fewest badges.

Many of our scouting activities involved going on long walks during which we would be taught the rudiments of pathfinding and tracking, which all enjoyed. When walking in single file the leader would often start singing, usually beginning with 'This old man he played one, he played knick-knack on my thumb'; followed by, 'Satu orang pegi, pegi padang lalang, satu orang sama anjing pegi padang lalang. Dua orang pegi.' and so on up to ten in Indonesian sung to the tune of 'One man went to mow.' We also enjoyed camping. This involved carrying our own canvas tents which were heavy but waterproof, and fresh water in army style khaki bottles strapped to the waist, as well as food, cooking pots and utensils. It was essential to set up camp near a fast-flowing stream so that if the worst came to the worst we could always boil the water from the stream should it be necessary. There was a curious phenomenon that happened at nights. When the sun had finally sunk below the horizon and when it should have been pitch dark the whole area was lit by phosphorescence that seemed somehow to settle on dead wood. It was easy to tell which branches of a tree were dead but had not yet fallen because of this wonderful luminescence. At the base of each tree was a myriad of sparkling twigs and branches that lit up the area around for a hundred feet or more. Millions of fireflies added to the shimmering world. They were like a swarm in an ever-changing shape as they flew around us, to join together again once they had passed. At night the whole effect was like an incandescent picture where unknown small animals scampered to and fro like vague silhouettes in the background.

We rose from our tents with the dawn, around 6 am, and everyone had a turn in cooking a meal, two of us at a time. Breakfast nearly always consisted of scrambled eggs cooked in pitch-black frying pans which looked as though they had never been washed. It did not matter how badly the meal was cooked, it was always delicious, nothing was wasted and we were always hungry. These were the occasions when we used to eat the bark from the cinnamon trees.

Once a year at the end of the winter term the scout troop put on a display for the benefit of the school and any parents who could come. Because of the distance most parents had to journey, those who were able to attend mainly came from Singapore. The display was always very varied, but the highlight was the building of a bridge over an imaginary river. Two teams took part and speed was essential. The team that won usually had the strongest boys. At the last of these displays, before Japan entered the Second World War in December 1941, another boy from the Wolf Patrol and I were to give a demonstration of fighting with quarter staffs. We had succeeded in building up a very fast routine of attacks and parries which really did look as though we were having a genuine fight. Unfortunately, when the time came, I forgot to parry an attacking stroke and my opponent brought his staff hard down on my head. The staff broke into three pieces, my face was cut open and all my front teeth knocked loose. When I regained consciousness, one of the boys took me to hospital to have my face seen to. My cheek needed to be stitched, but the hospital was very low on anaesthetics of any kind and it was essential for them to keep what little they had for real emergencies. They strapped me to the operating table and placed a rubber sheet over my head and chest. The sheet had a hole in it large enough for the doctor to see what he was doing and a clamp was secured either side of my head and over my forehead to immobilize me. Until the stitching started I was blissfully unaware that there was not to be an anaesthetic. I screamed in pain – they must have heard me at the school. I had six stitches in all and when the operation was finished a large plaster was placed over much of the left side of my face. It was not until I returned to England that I was able to tell mother what had happened and then only because she asked how I got the scar on my face.

On the evening of my accident I had expected to sing the part of the Page, as a solo, in Good King Wenceslas, as my voice had not yet broken. The Christmas Show was for the benefit of the parents and also the pupils before the end of term. Since a large plaster covered much of my face, my stand-in had to take the part . As he sang, his voice started to break, which caused a lot of amusement.

Outings

With two terms of roughly four to five months the school allowed us a short holiday half way through each term. The first in the year was at Easter and the other during the second half of September. They lasted about three days. On these occasions we were taken on organised outings, two of which I remember vividly. The first was a visit to Medan Zoo at the end of April 1940 where we saw the world's largest monkey, an orang-outang named King Kong. The orang-outang is a native of Sumatra and lives in the forests. King Kong was enormous, and very frightening to look at. He was housed in a large cage behind thick steel bars and visitors were kept well back as he sometimes became very bad-tempered. In the cage he had a heavy steel ball and a thick metal plate rather like a discus, which were presumably put there for him to play with. While some of us watched, King Kong picked up the steel ball and in a fury flung it at us with such force that it actually went through the bars, but fortunately, just dropped outside the cage. This appeared to infuriate him even more, so picking up the plate he threw that as well. The plate went straight through the bars and disappeared into trees not far away. Anyone in the way could have been seriously injured. We were told that when the Japanese started to bomb Medan, King Kong had to be destroyed: if he had got loose he could have created havoc.

The other holiday, also at Easter the following year, was in every way a disaster. The intention was to take a coach trip to Lake Toba for a swim and a picnic. Not everyone wished to go but there were enough of us to fill two coaches, with a teacher to supervise in each. Lake Toba, the largest lake in south east Asia, was formed around one hundred thousand years ago by what was probably the world's greatest explosion, and lies in the world's biggest volcanic crater. It is situated in a valley between two parallel folded chains of mountains called the Bukit Barisan. The valley is broken up into separate sections by a series of volcanoes between which lie a string of lakes. Lake Toba is by far the largest nearly sixty miles long and nineteen miles wide, very deep with a large island, Samosir, in the middle.

We set off early morning as we would be picnicking on the lake shore near Prapat about sixty miles from school. The road wound its way through beautiful countryside where many trees are the same as in Britain: oak, chestnut and pine. In addition there are camphor trees, sandalwood, rubber, ironwood, banyan, mahogany, teak and ebony trees. Apart from the forest there are extensive areas of coarse grass; bamboo eight inches in diameter and more, grows everywhere in huge clumps; palm trees are common. Many varieties of wild orchid grow in the damp tropical conditions. Frangipani, and the blooms of the rhododendrons, are beautiful and enormous. Animals such as the elephant, rhinoceros, tiger, tapir and Malayan bear, the orang-outang, macaque gibbon and silver leaf monkey and also fruit bats live in Sumatra, but apart from the monkeys and bats we never saw any of these creatures in Kaban Djahe. What we did see were lovely plumed birds, various pheasants, Malay parrot, hornbill, woodpeckers and red breasted bee-eaters. There were also many species of magnificent butterflies, but my favourite was the Atlas Moth, the world's largest moth.

Unfortunately, this trip was suddenly marred. The leading coach overtook two cyclists riding one behind the other. Suddenly, for no apparent reason, the second cyclist shot out into the centre of the road when the first coach had overtaken him and was run down by the coach I was on. It happened in a flash. Our driver stopped, so did the first coach and the other cyclist. Everyone got out. The cyclist was dead. Not a lot was said. The surviving cyclist did not appear to be very upset and seemed to accept that what had happened could have occurred at any time, but for those who remained, life must still go on. Our driver helped lift the corpse to the side of the road while the dead man's friend cycled off to advise the authorities of what had happened. Returning to the coaches we drove on, a much subdued group of children with hardly a word spoken: with our own thoughts and anxieties, some with tears in their eyes.

We arrived at the lakeside and unloaded the picnic. We spread ground sheets on the earth, most of which was pumice, and set out the food on an assortment of dishes. Originally we had intended to swim before lunch but the delay had upset our programme so lunch came first. Not surprisingly it was a quiet lunch and some food remained uneaten, which was most unusual. When the meal was over some boys, including me, picked up large pieces of pumice, which was everywhere, and threw them into the lake where they made a plop and floated away propelled by the breeze. The girls had decided not to swim but I and others put on our bathing trunks. We were about to get into the water when a dead dog floated by, its belly grossly distended. The dog was followed by a dead donkey. No one went into the water; we all dressed and the two teachers decided it was time to return to school. The picnic cleared up, we returned to the coaches and drove back to Kaban Djahe.

The double line of trees below which we held our end of term lunch were garlanded with liana vines and where no vines were growing, ropes had been attached to the higher branches. When I and a group of friends had nothing better to do we would climb and swing from tree to tree, doing our best to imitate Tarzan. It was exhilarating: each swing could cover 50 feet and the double line of trees extended for over 200 yards. The lowest point of each swing came within 6 feet of the ground so should we fail to reach the next tree it was easy to get off and to start again.

The headmaster, Mr. Cookson was a butterfly enthusiast and had a wonderful collection, including what was reputed to be the largest Atlas Moth ever found in Sumatra, with a wing span exceeding 12 inches. He told me it was dead when he found it. The Atlas Moth is a native of Sumatra. The caterpillar is lime green in colour and grows to about 4 inches in length. As a chrysalis it hangs as a beautiful silken bobbin until it emerges as a moth ready for flight. Breaking out of the chrysalis can take an hour or two by which time it is exhausted so that it remains in the tree, slowly spreading and closing its wings to strengthen its muscles. Its initial flight almost always ends in disaster as it flops to the ground exhausted by the attempt. However, after further exercising of the wings it succeeds in taking to the air in a rather ungainly fashion to return to a nearby tree. Fully developed, the Atlas Moth is richly patterned in various shades of brown with curved forewing tips each with a red flash.

The forewings and hindwings have triangular translucent patches and the latter have brown spots joined together like a chain formation along the edge of the two wings. An irregular red line runs from fore to hind wings dividing each roughly in two. The very same trees that we used for our Tarzan exploits were also home to the Atlas Moth. Many were the times I gently pushed a finger under one of these moths when on the ground for it to climb on and remain there until ready for flight.

It was May 1940, shortly before the end of term that the school was treated to a wonderful show of magic put on by an Indian. Three large trestle tables had been arranged on the hockey pitch in the form of three sides of a square. The pupils sat on the ground in front of the open end of the square, in the middle of which was the magician and his young daughter, his assistant. The table on our left was covered in dolls of varying shapes and sizes all lying down. On the right table were placed a number of glasses each containing a coin, with a further coin placed outside each glass. The table at the rear held the magicians baggage under which was a large circular flat-topped basket tied up with rope. Taking a musical instrument, the kind commonly used by snake charmers, he played a rather ghastly tune and the dolls rose up and danced to and fro; on stopping they lay down again. Turning to the glasses he again played and the coins rose up on their circumference and slowly but surely rolled up the side of the glass and then down the other side, so they had exchanged places. The most spectacular turn was when he built up a pile of sticks around his assistant so that she could not be seen, and then set fire to it. A gasp of amazement could be heard as nothing was left but a pile of cinders. After a few more turns the magician pulled the large, flat-topped basket from beneath the table behind him and proceeded to untie it. Removing the cords and the lid the magician helped his assistant, who was tied hand and foot, out of the basket none the worse for her ordeal.

War in Europe

At school we were always kept up to date with World News, so on the fateful day at 6.15 pm Indonesian time on 3rd September 1939 the whole school had assembled in the Hall to listen to the speech by the Prime Minister, The Right Honourable Neville Chamberlain. It was getting dark and the Hall lights were on. The wireless was a brown, bakelite, table model, that was common at the time. I tried unsuccessfully to use the cat's whisker crystal set and earphones given to me by my parents. Although I did succeed in catching the occasional word when using the cat's whisker I could not keep it tuned to any station. We listened to the speech in a silence that continued after the broadcast had ended. Mr. Cookson rose, walked to the end of the Hall and mounted the dais. He elaborated on the consequences that might follow. Although, we in the Far East were not directly involved, our parents, and in particular our fathers might feel they should return to Britain to join up. Some years later I was to learn that my father had tried to return to England but had been prevented by the Company, as his work in Bangkok was considered to be of national importance in view of the teak required for ship building, munition boxes, lorry bodies, camp equipment and other uses. The talk over, Mr. Cookson announced that the film 'Edison the Boy' would be shown the following evening. I was very moved by the film and believe it will always remain one of the three films I have enjoyed most. Even as a young boy Edison was very inventive; playing out in the garden his mother told him to shut the upstairs window; he simply moved near to the wall directly beneath the window, which was two stories up, pulled a string and the window came crashing down; unfortunately the glass shattered which did not please his mother. He taught his sister the morse code which was to save the lives of all on a train that was fast approaching a bridge that had been swept away by floods. There were many other incidents demonstrating his inventiveness.

In September 1939 the British living in Bangkok numbered around 300 and together with about 2000 German civilians. On my return home to my parents in Bangkok for the Christmas holidays of the same year my parents gave me a number of badges which I proudly wore. One was a Spitfire, another V for Victory. Wearing these badges by the British upset the Germans in Bangkok and complaints were made by the German legation to the British Consulate. This only delighted the British who continued to wear their badges with pride.

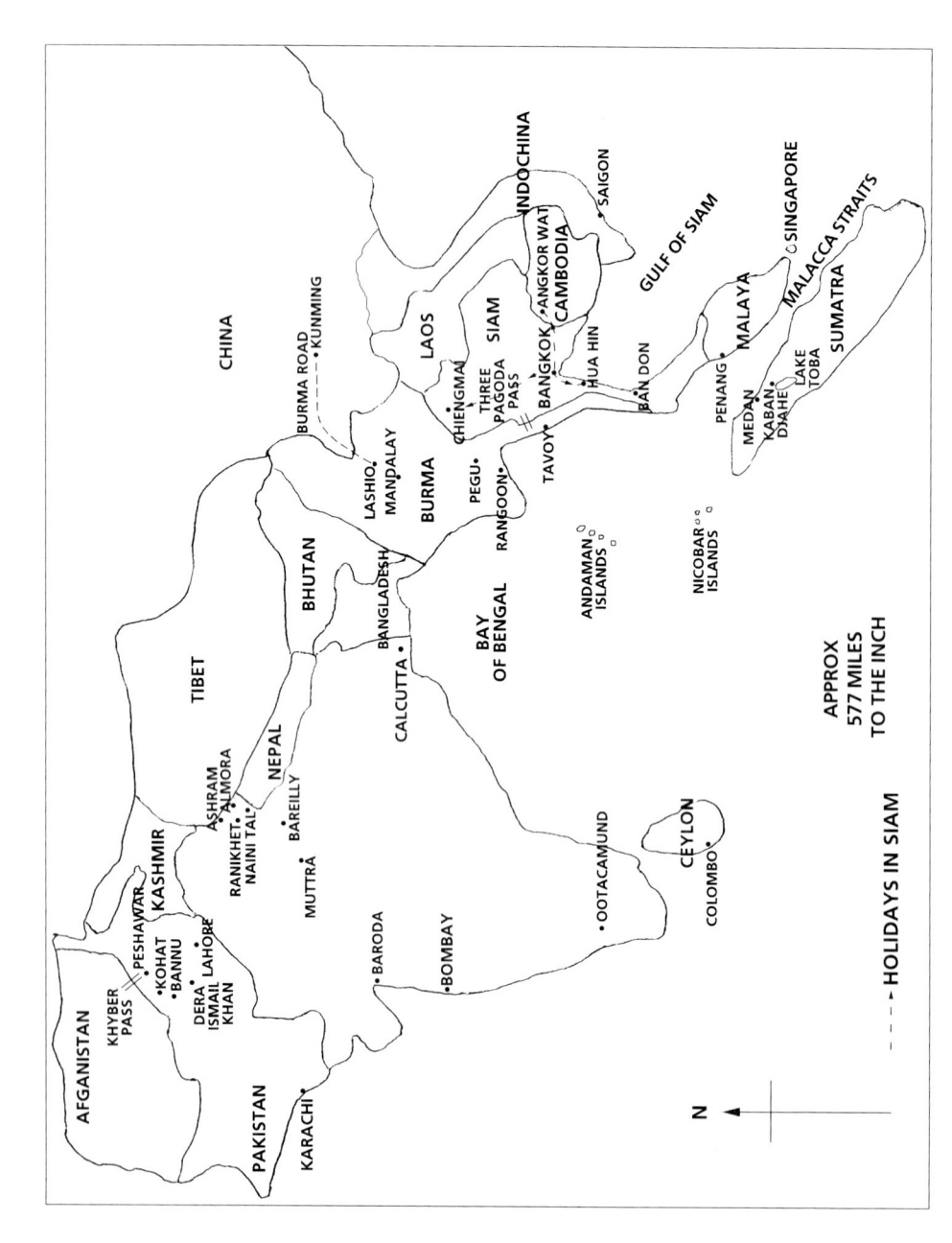

HOLIDAYS IN SIAM

Chapter 8.

Holidays in Siam

When I returned to school my mother furnished me with a stout aluminium box roughly a foot square and four to five inches deep. She expected me to fill this box with as many avocado pears as it would hold for my journey back to Bangkok. The avocado pears grown in Sumatra were, for some reason, far tastier than those available in Siam and they could easily be bought in any of the street markets for next to nothing. On the flight back home there was a short refuelling stop at Penang where one of the aircrew always treated me to a soft drink. My parents and brother met me when the plane I was on touched down, at Don Muang airport, from where we drove home.

My father went to his office early every morning, arriving between 6.30 and 7.00. The official hours were from 7am to 4pm. Tiffin, or lunch, was served in the office dining room at midday. By this time it was so hot that Father had to put blotting paper beneath both arms as the sweat would otherwise smudge what he was writing. His office was situated on one side of the Menam River right opposite the saw mill on the other side.

Father was also interested in hydroponics, a method of growing plants in a chemical solution without soil, and grew excellent tomatoes, but nothing else by this method.

In Siam, the Festival of Kites was held every year on 27th March, and took place opposite our house in Lumpini Park. Kites were of every shape, size, and type from very small to huge. There were box kites, diamond-shaped kites, barrel-shaped kites, kites with five or six sides, kites with no tail and kites with tails twenty feet long. Many were in the shape of animals; my favourite was a frog roughly 8 feet in diameter. It took three people to get it to fly and two to guide it once airborne. Other kites were in the shapes of birds, butterflies and dragons. The string or cord, depending on the size of the kite, was

The King's Palace, Bangkok

covered in ground glass and the idea was to cross your cord with that of another kite, then with a sawing motion try to cut the opponent's cord. Whoever succeeded was declared the winner. The larger kites were not always the winners. Apart from the competition, kite flying is a popular pastime in Bangkok and weather permitting, there are always lots of people to be seen flying kites in the park.

Another annual event was a huge fair held, I believe, in the grounds of the King's Palace. It covered acres of land and supported all the traditional side shows, merry-go-rounds and stalls that are to be seen in British fairs. When darkness fell all the activities were illuminated by twinkling fairy lights as the fair continued well into the night. A destructive child by nature, my greatest pleasure was throwing wooden balls at shelves full of crockery to see how much I could smash.

Many people have enjoyed the musical 'The King and I' based on the book 'Anna and the King of Siam', which was so beautifully produced, and acted by Yul Brunner and Deborah Kerr. Well, Anna, (her surname was Leonowens in real life) was an English lady who was given the responsibility by King Chulalongkorn of Siam of educating his many children. Anna had a son of her own who, when grown to manhood, opened a men's outfitters in Bangkok. It was by Anna's son that my father had some of his suits tailored.

Bangkok is full of beautiful temples, but my favourite was Wat Po with its huge reclining figure of Buddha 46 metres long and 15 metres high, all covered in gold leaf. Apart from the huge and beautiful figure of Buddha, the gallery around the inner sanctuary held a spectacular array of early bronze Buddhas.

My father, despite the humid climate, was a keen sportsman winning many cups for golf, tennis and squash. He frequently won the annual singles tennis tournament held at the Royal Bangkok Sports Club and in 1939 beat the Japanese champion on his return journey from the Wimbledon Tennis Championship. The Siamese champion and my father then took on the Japanese number one and number three in a doubles which they also won. I felt proud of my father as he came off court to cheers from the English contingent watching the match.

Our back garden had a washing line. A wooden pole propped up against the back wall of the house supported the line when in use. This pole had been there for ages and no one took any notice of it until one day we found it had taken root and small shoots were beginning to form at the top of the pole where it formed the letter Y.

From time to time my parents had friends to dinner especially if they came from up country on a short visit, usually from Chiengmai. It was an opportunity for exchanging news and views. A visitor who seldom came to Bangkok if he could avoid it was J.H.Williams perhaps better known as 'Elephant Bill' and later to become Lt-Col. J.H.Williams O.B.E. in recognition for his services under Field Marshall Sir William Slim of the XIVth Army. I was never present at any of these dinners but used to eavesdrop when Elephant Bill was being entertained, as the news from Chiengmai was always fascinating.

For holidays the family usually went to Hua Hin, a seaside resort on the South Eastern coast overlooking the Gulf of Siam. We stayed at the Railway Hotel which was a short way from the beach and surrounded by hedges cut into the shapes of animals. I believe it was the only hotel in Hua Hin and the approach was up a drive under a topiary elephant expertly trimmed by the gardeners. In Siamese mythology passing beneath a elephant is a sign of good luck.

At the rear of the hotel, not far away from the jungle, a path led into the trees. The path was in fact a rock formation on which nothing grew, but on either side the overhanging trees formed a dense canopy blocking out all sunlight. One day, father and I decided to explore. I led, but almost as soon as we entered the trees the path petered out and sunshine gave way to almost total darkness as the jungle enveloped us. We had to wait for our eyes to get accustomed to the dark before continuing at a much slower rate trying to find a way through the thick undergrowth. While making my way between two trees I suddenly realised that I had walked into a huge spider's web and there right in front of me was an enormous spider. I do not know which of us was the more frightened, but it was the spider that reacted first by dropping to the ground, where my father killed it. I found it surprisingly difficult to extricate myself from the web, but by this time we had had enough of the jungle so returned to the sunshine, when my father noticed that my hair was covered in strands of the spider's web.

Approach to the Railway Hotel, Hua Hin

Every day the family went swimming; Mother and Jon remained within their depth while my father swam out a lot further, taking me on his shoulders. I could swim very well by myself but Father and I had a lot of fun together. There was hardly ever anyone else on the beach, with beautiful sands as far as one could see in either direction. The shore shelved very gently so at low tide the sea went out for hundreds of yards, ideal for Mother and Jon.

One day, when quite far out, my father gave a cry of pain and dropped me in the sea as he swam and then ran to the shore. Although we had not noticed them before, I suddenly realised that I was only inches away from a very large jelly fish, and as I looked there were many more stretched out in a long line swimming toward the shore. I turned and fled, swimming as fast as I could. My father's leg swelled up, but after a couple of days it was back to normal.

Me at Hua Hin

Examining father's foot after jellyfish sting, Hua Hin, 1935

In Hua Hin there was a very small, one-room museum. It mostly contained objects that had been picked up along the shore. Its only surprising exhibit was an enormous Japanese land crab attached to the end wall and over three feet across. It made a great impression on me and I have never seen the like of it since.

Jon and I were the proud owners of a large German electric train with a number of carriages. The engine had a light in front of the boiler but we had very few rails. So in the Spring of 1940 my father arranged for the saw mill to produce more track as well as miniature trees, lamposts, stations, tunnels, scenery and many other things, as well as a raised control unit from which to operate the layout. This was erected on the upstairs verandah, and at night with the track lit up and the train rushing through the stations with its light shining brightly, the whole effect was magic.

Needless to say the rails were set in teak, the stations and everything else were also made of teak. The Chinese operators of the saw mill were delighted to have a change in their daily routine and thoroughly enjoyed this new and unusual task. Like the rest of the family possessions the train set was presumably destroyed by the Japanese, but I would like to think that it was still being played with by a Siamese family.

In June 1939 I was invited to go sailing by two German brothers who owned a four-berth, sea going, Bermuda rigged yacht with an auxiliary engine. We sailed among islands in the Bight of Bangkok. The seabed around these islands shelves very gently so the yacht, which had a deep keel, could only be anchored between half and one mile from shore without being caught in the sand. This meant that having anchored the yacht we had to swim to the islands. The sea was very calm, not a ripple to be seen. Using goggles we watched the underwater life; the seabed was about fifteen feet below us and the water surprisingly clear, with small multi-coloured fish darting in and out of rocks while seaweed swayed backwards and forwards with the motion of the water. We had not come to admire marine life, but to swim to one of the uninhabited islands and have a picnic, which the brothers had brought in waterproof containers. They selected a particular island roughly half a mile from where we had anchored and where they knew there would be plenty of brushwood with which to make a fire. The two brothers swam one either side of me in case I got into trouble and we had the occasional stop for breath and to admire the marine life. From time to time I felt something tickling my feet and mentioned it to my companions. "Yes, it is a baby shark," said one of the brothers, "but don't worry, as it is getting shallower all the time as we near land it is most unlikely the parent shark will bother us." I did not feel re-assured but reach land we did and there was plenty of brushwood for the picnic. One of the brothers had a nasty scar down his back where he had been attacked by a shark, but he had managed to kill it with his sheath knife. After the picnic we swam back to the yacht. This was the only occasion I ever went out with the brothers and I spent three most enjoyable days sailing with them, and they never once had to use the auxiliary engine. When war broke out in Europe they returned to Germany to join the army.

Health hazards

In addition to sharks and the usual tropical diseases, there are other health hazards of living in the Far East so that it is essential to avoid taking risks. During the winter holiday of 1940 I caught pneumonia and was put to bed with six blankets over me. My chest was covered with a thick poltice of hot antiphlogistine, brown paper, and heavily bandaged. The outside temperature was around 85°F. The idea was to sweat it out and sweat it out I certainly did. The first night I had a nightmare with motorbikes tearing around a circular dirt track and crashing, with blood and bodies all over the place. Mother had a difficult few nights as I was delirious some of the time, until the fever broke and I recovered.

In early June 1940 I caught the calf of my right leg on a protruding nail while playing on the climbing frame in the garden. There was very little blood and I ignored the slight injury. The following day the whole area around the cut was bright red, so I showed it to my Mother. She was furious and called in the doctor. Apart from iodine and a plaster I don't know what he put on the cut, but it took six weeks to heal.

During the same holiday I also picked up a verruca on the ball of my right foot, probably from the swimming pool. It became very painful, and made it impossible to walk properly. Our doctor took it out with an electric needle. I did not feel the minor operation until the anaesthetic had worn off, then it was agony, so I sat in the garden with my foot level with, or higher than my head, to ease the pain, but for three days I had to use crutches to get around.

There were of course the usual inoculations against diseases such as cholera, typhoid, tuberculosis and vaccination against smallpox. I also avoided hookworm, dysentery and beriberi. Dengue fever was fairly common, but this I caught only once. Occasionally, mother would remove a tick that somehow managed to get on to my scalp. I think she did this with a strong pair of tweezers, but I may be wrong.

Once my leg had healed and my foot better I was allowed to sail on one of the Company ships to Singapore. As usual the ship was loaded with teak. The voyage normally took two days. Once into the Gulf of Siam the Captain said,

"How would you like to steer the ship?"

"I'd like to very much, but you'll have to show me what to do," I replied.

He took me to the bridge and introduced me to the helmsman who was at the wheel. I then took over; although I was familiar with the compass on land, it was necessary to concentrate to keep the vessel on course in rolling seas. In the meantime the Captain kept a lookout from the bridge. "It looks like we're in for a spot of trouble, the sea's getting up and the clouds are gathering." said the Captain. It was becoming more difficult for me to hold the wheel. "We're heading for a squall, change direction to East South East." said the Captain. Try as I might I could not turn the wheel to the new course. Suddenly a huge wave hit us broadside on, I lost my grip on the wheel and was thrown to one side of the Bridge. The wheel spun this way and that until stopped by the helmsman who steered the ship to face the oncoming waves. Speed was reduced while we rode out the squall which lasted about two hours. Meanwhile I had been unable to leave the Bridge for fear of being swept overboard.

We eventually berthed at Singapore some four to five hours later than anticipated. I disembarked and went to the Customs Office. The Officer examined my passport and papers. "You realise sonny that we cannot allow you to return to Bangkok until you have been re-vaccinated against Small Pox, it is now due again." This turned out to be a considerable nuisance as the vaccination did not take until the third attempt when a red swelling could be seen on my arm and I was then permitted to return to Siam.

It was during the same holiday that a Sunderland Flying Boat landed at Bangkok and for two weeks took visitors on an a sightseeing tour over the city. I went on one of the flights and asked the stewardess if I could fly the plane for a few minutes, as I had been allowed to do by K.N.I.L.M. but the answer was an emphatic, no. What I enjoyed most was the taking off and landing to see the spray which glistened like a rainbow as the sun shone through the droplets of water.

*Mother at the
BBTCL
Bungalow,
Chiengmai, 1938*

*Ayutthaya
on Menam River
about 40 miles
north of Bangkok*

Chapter 9

My last holiday in Siam

The family occasionally visited Chiengmai for a holiday, but only when father had some unfinished business to attend to. Our favourite holiday haunt was Hua Hin, south of Bangkok and facing on to the Gulf of Thailand with blue sea and wonderful beaches. Chiengmai was 'up country' about three hundred and eighty miles north of Bangkok. The vegetation was luxuriant and cooler than in the capital. My main interest were the elephants, they fascinated me and I spent many happy hours watching and feeding them. The town of Chiengmai, which is much more westernised than Bangkok, because of all the Europeans involved in the teak trade, is situated on the river Meping and is overlooked by the mountain Doi Sutep which rises, a short distance from the west bank of the river, to a height of five thousand feet. On the east bank were the offices and houses belonging to the Bombay Burma Trading Corporation. Typical of all towns and villages throughout Siam, Chiengmai had its fair share of mangy pi-dogs covered in sores and flies which roamed the streets looking for scraps. While there I would watch horse racing and cricket. There was also a gymkhana, but none of these activities did I find of interest as I was too young to take part.

The festival of umbrellas called Bo Sangumbrelle Fair and Sankampaeng Handicraft Festival was held during one of our visits. Many of the inhabitants and those from surrounding areas came with beautifully decorated umbrellas. I was fascinated by the wonderful colours depicting flowers, dragons and animals, it was a sheer delight.

Chiengmai is the heart of the teak growing area and where the Bombay Burmah Trading Corporation elephants were trained and kept in large stockades. Each day native employees of the company went into the jungle to cut down selected teak trees. The felling was done manually, one man at either end of a saw, for in those days there were no petrol-driven saws. When a tree had been felled, an elephant controlled by his oozie would arrive at the scene, dismount and secure chains around the log and to the elephant's harness. When ready, and instructed to do so, the elephant picked up his oozie with his trunk and placed him safely on his back. The elephant would now drag the log to the river bank. This was not as easy as it may sound. Sometimes a tree might be felled in a difficult position to get at or the ground could be particularly awkward to negotiate; occasionally it required two or more elephants to extract a tree. This could be achieved in a number of ways depending on the problem. I watched one elephant pulling with another pushing to move a large log. Where the ground is comparatively even, without too much debris lying around, the elephant would roll the log. Every action of the tusker would be controlled by its oozie. Once the chains had been removed the elephants dragged or pushed the logs to the river bank and then into the River Ping. In the water, they were left to float downstream where they would take weeks to reach Bangkok. After a hard day's work, the oozie took his elephant to the river for them both to have a much needed bath and to be scrubbed clean. Sometimes I was allowed to ride on an elephant sitting on a howdah and always accompanied by an adult. At first it felt strange, a kind of pitching motion rather like a small boat in a choppy sea, and I expected the howdah to fall off, but it never did. What I enjoyed more was when I could steal away on foot and join the oozies as they worked the gentle giants. Occasionally an oozie would order his elephant to pick me up and put me on its back. I was thrilled, but never told anyone in case I got into trouble.

As the Menam River flowed through Bangkok, I found that the best place to watch the whole process of securing the trees to the point where they were turned into planks, was from the side of the slide, and well out of harm's way. A flexible boom situated opposite the saw mill, trapped the logs. Agile natives would walk on the logs without falling into the river, not easy to do, as the logs had a habit of spinning around as soon as you stepped on them. Trying to keep their balance was a bit like a circus act. Their job was to guide each log to the side of the river where a chain would be secured and the log dragged up a slide into the saw mill. Fortunately accidents were few, but there was an occasion so I was told by father, when the electric rollers were accidentally switched on as they were being cleaned by an operative. The poor man was thrown forward into the teeth of a revolving bandsaw and lost an arm before he managed to get off.

Elephant and its oozie, Chiengmai 1938

From the slide onwards everything was mechanised. Cranes gripped the heavy logs and fed them into a series of band saws where they were cut into planks of wood. The thickness and size of a plank could be varied according to what was required. The bandsaws rotated at enormous speed passing through a tank of water to cool them down as they bit into the wood. Without the cooling process, the saws would overheat and snap. I frequently visited the mill to watch it in action and considering that teak is a hardwood I was continually amazed how these saws cut through the length of a tree as though it were made of butter.

The fragrant smell of the teak when the saws started cutting overpowered the pungent odour of the river with its rotting carcasses of dead animals that slowly drifted downstream. While the scent from the wood was pleasant, the noise of machinery was not: the clatter of the chains as the logs were pulled up the slide; the creaking of the pulleys as the cranes placed the logs on to the rollers; the bump, bump, bump, of the logs as they were fed toward the saws; the shutting of the clamps as they gripped the logs; the hissing of the saws as they bit into the wood, and finally the noise of the water as it struck the screens and dropped back into the tanks of water only to be caught up again in a continuous cycle, while at the far end the planks emerged steaming, due to the friction of the saws. Nobody spoke, it was impossible.

I had just returned home after my first term at Highlands School when my father decided to make a quick visit to see Angkor Wat in Cambodia and asked if I would like to go with him, to which I readily agreed. A friend had mentioned it was worth a visit, although covered in jungle. It was the end of June 1939 when we left Bangkok by train early in the morning. In this part of the world nothing moved very quickly, and especially not the trains. It took all day to reach Siemreap by which time it was almost dark. Angkor Wat is in the region of Siemreap, the site of the ruins of the capital of the Khmer Empire. The capital was founded in the 9th century and Angkor Wat built in 1140 AD and abandoned around 1440.

Having left the train, we caught a small boat which took us to the Wat. By this time the sun had set, but there was a beautiful moon which gave a romantic glow to the surrounding area. We did not have far to go when to my surprise I was looking up at an enormous figure of Buddha enveloped by thick creeper. As we travelled slowly along the river it was possible to make out the ruins of what had once been a magnificent city, and all this by moonlight. Trees had grown up in the open spaces while the ruined buildings were covered in creeper, some as much as nine inches thick. We saw fallen statues and monkeys chattered and swung from tree to tree as if to say "You are intruding on our domain." With the moonlight shining through the trees and sparkling on the ripples of water, it became a vision of delight. We must have spent about two hours in sheer amazement and for my part I just could not understand why it had all been abandoned to the jungle. After that the return journey to Bangkok was an anti-climax.

A ceremony, that has been held in Siam for many centuries, is known as the First Ploughing, or Raek Nah. It is celebrated in May and takes place on the outskirts of Bangkok in a spot reserved exclusively for this purpose. I had recently returned from school and father decided to attend. Cook produced a picnic hamper full of sandwiches, mangoes, mangosteens, pomelos and plenty to drink and we set off by car. As usual mother sat in front, with Jon and me in the back. Because of the humid weather all the windows were lowered, but it made little difference as the road was crowded with bicycles, richshaws, cars and people and it took over an hour to reach the field. The only relief to an unpleasant journey and the dismal weather were the occasional groups of Siamese ladies we saw, dressed in beautiful, gaily coloured sarongs.

It was quite late in the morning before most people had arrived and the ceremony commenced. In the middle of the field were three tall bamboo poles from which hung four coloured paper lanterns to each pole. In one corner of the field in a small hut, stood various altars and figures of Buddha, where a number of priests were chanting prayers. What looked to me like two large tents had been erected on one side of the field, one for the Royal Family and the other tent for members of the royal household.

After a while a military band appeared followed by someone blowing a horn which made a curious sound, but typical of Siam. The band was followed by warriors in brightly-coloured uniforms and the King, carried in a chair on the shoulders of four men. The King was taken to the hut where the priests were chanting. What happened there I was not tall enough to see. By this time we were all getting hungry and thirsty, so we tucked into our picnic.

While the King was in attendance at the altars, two oxen covered in red and gold cloth, and harnessed to a large and highly decorated plough, were brought into the field and commenced making furrows in the earth. The King, having finished his prayers, came over to where the oxen were ploughing and was given some seeds which he scattered on the ground. He was followed by an official, probably a priest, who sprinkled holy water over the seeds. Once again my view was blocked, but father kept Jon and me informed of what was going on. The oxen were released from their harness and led to what looked like troughs each containing a different kind of seed. Whichever seed the oxen appeared to favour was chosen as being the best for the next year. The selection having been made by the oxen the place went mad with excitement. Father thought it was a good time to make for home so as to avoid the crush; he was right.

My last holiday in Bangkok and what turned out to be the last occasion I would see my father, was the summer of 1941. Leslie, my father, had always been keen on the idea of sailing home to England with the family in his own sea-going yacht. He received a yachting magazine on a monthly basis which he studied assiduously. As usual my parents and Jon met me at the airport on my return home. Father asked me to sit in the front seat of the car next to him, which was most unusual. "I am proposing to build a yacht with an auxiliary engine," he said, "and when we arrive home you will see my plan drawn out in chalk on the upstair verandah," he continued. "I thought that during your holidays we could go through the details together and I would welcome your ideas if you have any. The yacht will be built in the mill and made of teak with brass fittings."

When we arrived home I dashed upstairs to see the layout and was most impressed. There were to be four berths, two toward the bow for Jon and myself, separated by a door, and two amidships for mother and father. The forward cabin was smaller than my parents', the bunks slightly shorter and with less headroom. I would also be unable to stand upright in the cabin, but it all looked very cosy. The galley would be toward the stern, under cover, but separated from the sleeping quarters by a door. Inside the cabin, where my parents were to sleep and where we could all stand upright, was a built-in WC, basin and shower. Above and below the bunks were built-in cupboards; no space was wasted and there would be ample room for food and stores of all kinds. Behind one of the panels was a large storage tank for fresh water which would be piped to the galley sink. The flooring amidships would be secure but not fixed so that it could be removed by pulling on a brass ring, if for any reason it was necessary to get to the engine. Even so father intended to sail slowly and to put in to port on many occasions for fresh supplies and to have a general look around places of interest.

"As it will be a sea-going yacht I assume it will have a deep keel?" I said, to my father.

"Yes," he replied.

"And will it be retractable?"

"No, I am not in favour of a retractable keel in a sea going yacht, it is too risky."

"And what kind of rig will you have?" I asked, as I was thinking about the sea-going yacht that I had sailed on with the German brothers in 1939.

"The yacht will have a tall mast and Bermuda Rig with a triangular jib and a large triangular mainsail which will make it easy to handle as I do not want to use the engine except in an emergency," Father answered. "I anticipate it will cost in the order of £2,000."

Father had planned to sail down the East coast of Africa around the Cape of Good Hope, up the West side of Africa and so on past Portugal and France to England. In all it should take six months. Apart from crossing the Indian Ocean, we would never be far from land. All this was to be achieved when the war in Europe was over. Little did he expect a war in the Far East. Had his hopes come to fruition he expected to sell the yacht for about £24,000, as a colleague of his had done before the commencement of World War 2.

Chapter 10

War in the Far East

In the months leading up to Japan entering the war, it was curious – though it might have been coincidental – many Japanese left Indonesia. One such person known to us was the school photographer. He had been noticed taking photographs of the surrounding area which was not his usual habit. It was when Mr. Cookson said shortly before the end of term, when we were all assembled in the Hall, "There will be no school photograph this year as Mr. Hiroaki, I am reliably informed, has apparently returned to Japan without letting me know. Please convey my apologies to your parents and tell them that I hope to have found a suitable replacement photographer by the time you all return in January." I have never liked being photographed so was pleasantly surprised by this announcement.

I had just turned thirteen. The war in the Far East came as a great shock to me and all at the school. Our teachers told us that the Japanese had bombed Pearl Harbour and there were many dead and injured, not to mention the destruction of the U.S. Pacific fleet. It was the 7th December 1941 and term had just ended. Many of my friends left for home the same day and I was looking forward to leaving on the 8th. The 8th December arrived and all the pupils, except me, said goodbye. I believe that the Cooksons' three daughters had already returned to the U.S.A. My flight back to Bangkok had been cancelled. The Japanese had officially declared war, but already had their troops on the Siam/Burma and Siam/Malay borders, having infiltrated before war was declared. So here I was alone with a few of the teachers who had not yet left for their homes. At first I simply wandered around expecting to go home at any moment, but the moment never came. Mr. Cookson explained to me what had happened but could give me no news of my parents or brother. (Fifty years later I discovered that Mr.Streatfeild, the Bangkok manager of Bombay Burma Trading Corporation, had ordered my father not to leave Bangkok if he valued his job).

By the middle of the month all the teachers had left apart from Mr. and Mrs. Cookson and Miss L.M. Smith. Living in Kaban Djahe at the time were Mr. and Mrs.Yates and Mr. and Mrs.White. There was still no news of my family. Mr. Cookson asked me to stay with him and his wife in their house in the school grounds. As the only pupil there was little point in my remaining in a dormitory for twelve children. Shortly before Christmas Mr. Cookson received a telegram from the Bombay Burma Trading Corporation requesting that I should be evacuated as soon as possible to Rangoon. So it seemed that at last I would meet my family in Burma, or so I thought. Christmas Day arrived; there were no festivities, only a kind of foreboding in the air. Mrs. Cookson did her best to make it a happy occasion. There was a Christmas tree with decorations and fairy lights and she gave me a present of the card game 'Happy Families.'

At the end of December the Dutch Army took over some of the school buildings for their Headquarters in northern Sumatra. The troops were led by Col. George Frank Victor Gosenson "Ridder in de Militaire Ordre nr.4" the Dutch equivalent of the British VC. which he was awarded in 1920 for outstanding bravery while fighting in Aceh. He was born in Bandjermasin, Borneo in May 1888.

One morning early in January 1942, I awoke to find the games fields were being covered in a forest of bamboo stakes each about 12 feet long and set 12 feet apart, one end sharpened to an arrowhead, together with barb, and fixed in the ground at varying angles. The idea was to deter Japanese parachutists from landing. It was not only the school playing fields that were being staked but all open spaces.

At last something interesting was happening. The troops marched, exercised and trained daily, but the only guns they had were carbines. Col. Gosenson also interested me: of medium height, stocky, with silver grey hair, he was always immaculately dressed in his uniform; his Sam Browne was so highly polished it reflected the sunlight. Rows of medals hung against his chest, and from his side a long sword in a silver scabbard. He and his aide-de-camp both rode magnificent horses in and out of the forest of stakes. One day I picked up sufficient courage to say to Col. Gosenson,

"How did you get that scar on your face?"

He smiled, "While I was leading a platoon of men into battle in Aceh in 1917. It was hand-to-hand fighting and I was struck with a klewang. A fellow soldier and I had to hold up the lower part of my face while we made our way to an army truck not far away when I was able to lie down. The journey took two hours to our nearest field hospital where I received treatment."

"Gosh," I said, "It must have been dreadfully painful."

"Much of the time I was unconscious." he replied.

Col. Gosenson and his troops continued fighting the Japanese after the capitulation of Sumatra but was caught at the end of March 1942. While in captivity he took part in 'underground' operations against the Japanese until the plot was discovered. He was shot by the Japanese on 9th. January 1945 at Fort de Kock, now Bukittinggi.

We were having breakfast one morning early in January when Mr. Cookson said "When you have finished your tea I would like you to go to your room and pack the small blue KLM case under your bed with a change of clothing and any small possessions you wish to take. Last night, I had a phone call from KNILM in Medan to say they could accomodate you on a flight to Rangoon this afternoon. As you know the bus leaves the school gates at 10 am and you must be on it." I went to my room and the first thing that went into the case was my stamp album in the middle right at the bottom. After years of experience of going through Customs I was sure they would only feel down the corners of the case and not bother about the middle. If they should find the album it would be confiscated. On top of the album I placed a pair of shorts, shirt, vest and pants and down the corners I pushed in socks and handkerchiefs; by then the case was full and I locked it. At five minutes to 10 am I said goodbye to Mr. and Mrs. Cookson, thanked them for taking care of me, wished them well and caught the bus which for once was on time. As we drove I wondered if I would ever again travel this road with its many hairpin bends and overhanging ramps, with the occasional lorry or bus that had shot over the corner because of brake failure caught in trees twenty feet or so below. The monkeys swung from tree to tree and fled at the noise of an approaching vehicle. Whoever was employed to build this road had been paid by the kilometre so had done his best to make it as long as possible.

We stopped at Brastagi as usual to pick up passengers for Medan where we arrived two hours later. I changed buses as I had done many times before and shortly arrived at the airport where I booked in. Soon it was my turn to go through Customs, so pretending my case was as light as a feather I placed it on the table, unlocked it, opened the lid and turned it to face the Customs Officer. True to form he carefully felt down the corners of the case without disturbing the top, closed the lid and with a chalk placed a large tick on top. I turned the case around to face me and locked it. Just to show how light it was I carried it into the departure lounge with one finger in case the Officer had second thoughts. I was surprised to see so few people, usually it was busy. Of course I would be flying to Rangoon, whereas in peacetime the plane would be going to Singapore, or in my case to Bangkok, via Penang. Then I started to think: how could the plane reach Rangoon as it would normally have to make re-fuelling stops which were now being attacked, if not already overrun, by the Japanese? I gave up thinking about it and assumed that the aircraft had sufficient fuel capacity to reach Rangoon. I got a glass of water from the bar and sat down in one of the armchairs to wait.

There was little activity at the airport. A KNILM plane stood on the runway where a few cases were being loaded from a trolley into the plane's fuselage. I assumed that this was the plane I would be on. Half an hour went by and nothing appeared to be happening so I got out of my chair and strolled around, occasionally gazing out of the windows to see if there was any further activity.

Two hours later a large group of around thirty well-dressed men and a few women arrived and sat down. It was shortly after the arrival of this group that an airport official approached me and said, "You will have to return to your school; the plane is full up and will not now be going to Rangoon. I have told your Headmaster by phone that you will be returning." I was dumbfounded, but there was nothing else for me to do. On my return, the Cooksons were most sympathetic and so I was once more back in the old routine, not knowing what was to happen to me and still no news of my family.

January passed slowly. The Japanese army was sweeping through Malaya and their troops had landed in the Southern half of Sumatra and were racing northwards toward Medan. There was nothing to stop them as I believe the Dutch Army were not equipped with heavy artillery. Meanwhile troops under the command of Col. Gosenson had commenced digging trenches along the roadsides and various other places of strategic importance. When I next met the Colonel I said, "Why are you digging trenches, isn't it a waste of time?" Leaning from his horse he looked down at me and said, "The Japanese know there is nothing to bomb in Kaban Djahe so instead they will machine gun people walking along roads and wherever they see them. The trenches are for the protection of the civilians."

By the middle of the month I was at a loose end, bored, fed up, and disappointed at being unable to join my family in Rangoon. I walked around in a kind of daze; nothing was happening, my friends had all gone home and were probably having a lovely holiday, while I was stuck unable to go anywhere. My occasional chats with Col. Gosenson became fewer and fewer and I missed watching him ride through the stakes of bamboo. Apart from mealtimes, when Mr. Cookson kept me up to date with the news, he and his wife were busy, presumably preparing for the Spring Term. I wandered to the shops, talked briefly to one or two of the shopkeepers, and strolled around in the vain hope I would find something constructive to do. Every day was the same. Inwardly I was most concerned as to the fate of my parents as I had had no news from, or about them. I was not even sure they were in Rangoon.

It was toward the end of the month that I began to realise what war was really about. One morning I was walking back to school, having gone to buy a few sweets in town, when the earth all round me started to fly in every direction; it was immediately followed by the noise of a machine gun. I looked up as a plane shot past, its engines cut; I just had time to notice the rising sun emblem on the wings. The Japanese fighter planes became frequent visitors to Kaban Djahe. Col. Gosenson told me they were Mitsubishi A6M Zeke single seater fighters. The pilots had a habit of flying high, then they cut the engine and with the sun behind them and machine guns blazing would swoop down firing at anyone out in the open, just as the colonel had predicted.

By now I had been reduced to spending much of my time in the hideout which my school friends and I had made during my first term, in the thick hedge near the main gate of the school. Mr. Cookson had lent me three books to read; they were 'With Clive in India,' by G.H.Henty, 'The Long Traverse,' by John Buchan, and 'Kim' by Rudyard Kipling. As I had already read 'The Jungle Book' by Rudyard Kipling and thoroughly enjoyed it, I decided to read 'Kim,' which I loved. 'Clive of India' sounded a bit stuffy to me so I started 'The Long Traverse,' but fate decreed that I was not to finish it.

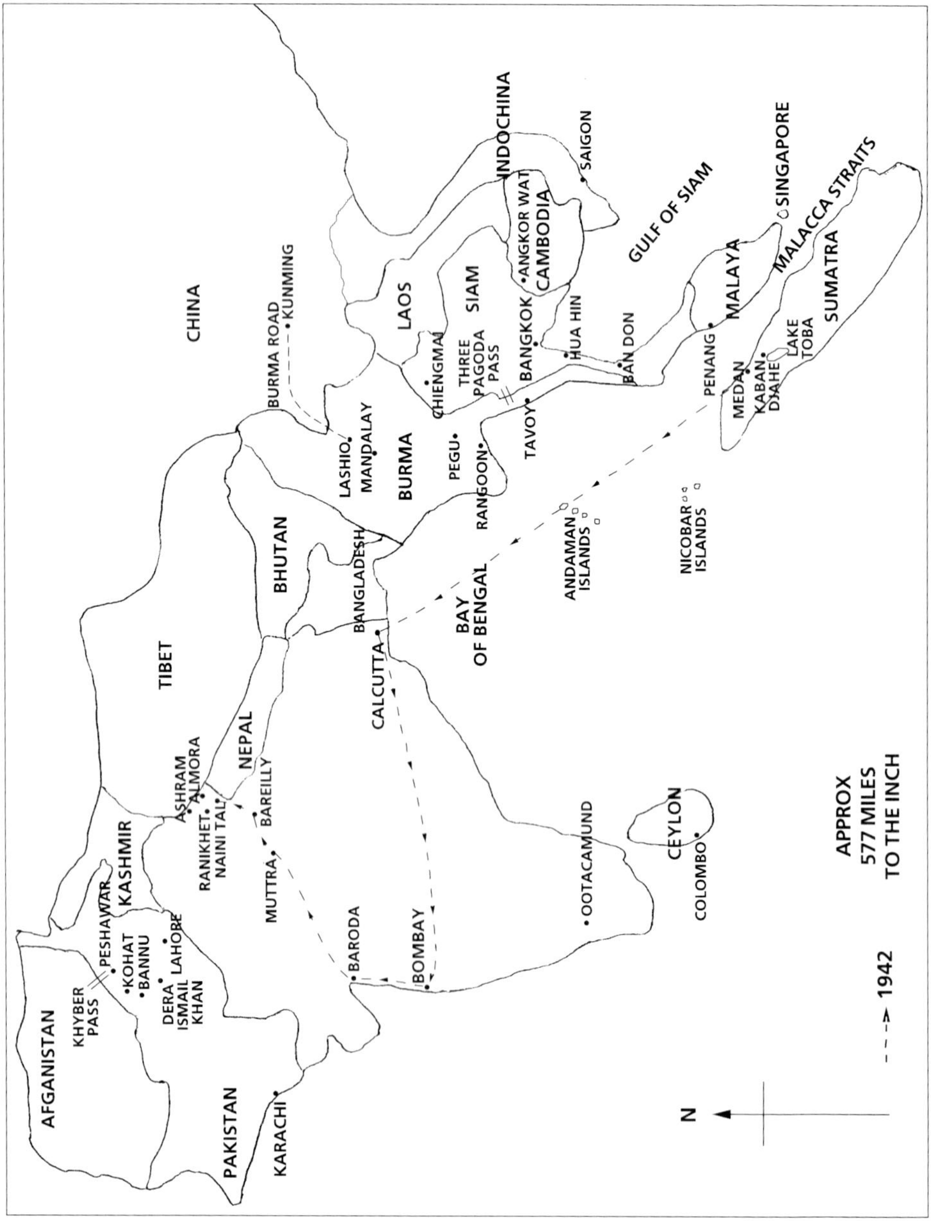

AFGANISTAN
KHYBER PASS
PESHAWAR
KOHAT
BANNU
DERA ISMAIL KHAN
LAHORE
PAKISTAN
KARACHI
KASHMIR
TIBET
ASHRAM
ALMORA
RANIKHET
NAINI TAL
NEPAL
BAREILLY
MUTTRA
BARODA
BOMBAY
CALCUTTA
BHUTAN
BANGLADESH
BAY OF BENGAL
OOTACAMUND
CEYLON
COLOMBO
CHINA
BURMA ROAD
KUNMING
LASHIO
MANDALAY
BURMA
PEGU
RANGOON
TAVOY
ANDAMAN ISLANDS
NICOBAR ISLANDS
LAOS
CHIENGMAI
THREE PAGODA PASS
SIAM
BANGKOK
HUA HIN
BAN DON
ANGKOR WAT
CAMBODIA
INDOCHINA
SAIGON
GULF OF SIAM
PENANG
MALAYA
MEDAN
KABAN DJAHE
LAKE TOBA
SUMATRA
MALACCA STRAITS
SINGAPORE
APPROX 577 MILES TO THE INCH
1942
N

Chapter 11

Out of Sumatra

There was nothing in particular for me to do during the next few weeks. I visited the natives who kept guard over the sugar cane plantation and they gave me a stick to chew. I peeled off the outer covering and chewed the inner core which is delicious, then spat out the pith. Another day I visited the corn plantation and was given corn on the cob that had just ripened. There was no need for butter, it was so fresh it could not have been bettered.

Everywhere I went there was an air of apprehension, like a dark cloud looming on the horizon waiting for the storm to break. Small groups of people gathered by the roadside or in shops. There was only one topic of conversation, the war. Everyone knew the Japanese had landed in southern Sumatra and were working their way north; there was nothing to stop them. Tales of torture and rape had already reached Kaban Djahe. Some of the shops had already been boarded up, and the inhabitants, reluctant to leave their possessions behind, were drifting toward the forests, in a vain hope of avoiding the enemy.

One night, while at supper with Mr. and Mrs. Cookson, I said,
"What are you going to do about the Japanese invasion, are you going to leave before they arrive?"

Mr. Cookson replied, "This is our house and our school, we started here three years ago and we regard it as our home. We shall not be leaving but hope the Japanese will leave us alone as we are civilians and are not armed."

"If I can't get away can I stay with you?" I said.

"Of course you can," said Mrs. Cookson. "We would be glad of your company."

I sighed with relief, and thought to myself that at least I would be with two people I knew well and hoped that when the war was over, I would be re-united with my parents.

In the days that followed I and many others walked around looking up at the skies and not paying much attention to what was going on on the ground. In any event Kaban Djahe was never noted for its traffic and what little there was could be heard long before it could be seen. The occasional Japanese fighter flew over and strafed roads and buildings and inevitably there were injuries, but most people got used to the idea of jumping into trenches whenever enemy aircraft were around. To the best of my knowledge there was no bombing in the north of Sumatra as there were no strategic installations of any kind.

I kept my suitcase packed in the vague hope that one day I might be able to leave. The British Vice-consul in Medan at this time was Sir Gordon Witteridge and a friend of my mother. She had asked him to keep an eye on me while at school in Kaban Djahe and I have every reason to believe that he was instrumental in my eventual escape from Sumatra. Sir Gordon himself did not leave Sumatra until the 19th February 1942. Tragically he had arranged for his wife and two daughters to leave by boat a month earlier, but the ship was sunk by the Japanese with the loss of all hands.

Early in the morning of the 9th February I was awakened by someone gently shaking my shoulder. "Wake up," said Mr. Cookson "You have five minutes to dress, my wife is making you some sandwiches and I have arranged for you to travel by lorry to Medan as there is no time to wait for a bus – speed is essential; it will probably be your last chance to get out of Sumatra. There is a plane going to Rangoon if they can get it ready in time." It took me barely a minute to dress and after I said a quick goodbye to Mrs. Cookson, Mr. Cookson and I were racing to the school gates. There waiting, engine running, was an open lorry filled with red chillis. I jumped in next to the driver and Mr. Cookson handed me my suitcase. "Goodbye!" I shouted, "Please thank Mrs. Cookson for the sandwiches," and off we drove.

That was the last time I saw Mr W. Stanley Cooksons BA JP or his wife Mrs W. S. Cookson BA. In trying to bring together the strands of this story, I found out later through Stichting Noord Sumatra Documentatie that both Mr. and Mrs. Cookson were caught by the Japanese and interned, and so were Miss Smith, who was a teacher at Highlands School, Mr. and Mrs.Yates and Mr. and Mrs. White who were living in Kaban Djahe at the time. Initially they were interned in Kaban Djahe. Sometime later the British internees were taken to Brastagi to join the Dutch prisoners and finally they were all taken to Aek Paminke next to Bandar Durian about 30 kilometres north of Rantau Prapat. This camp was devoid of any comfort, no water, no electricity, no wood for cooking, no paved roads, etc. Whether they survived their ordeal I have not been able to discover.

My driver to Medan, who seemed rather quiet, made me feel uneasy. As I was reasonably conversant in Indonesian I asked him what was the latest news. He was very worried, because of the rumours which were rife about the Japanese atrocities, the killing of civilian men and the raping of their wives and daughters. He was concerned as to what would happen to him and his family when the Japanese reached Kaban Djahe. He told me that the southern outskirts of Medan were already being shelled and he believed it would not be long before the city fell. Japanese fighter planes regularly strafed anything that moved on the ground.

After about twenty minutes in the lorry my eyes began to run with tears – the chillis were the problem and my head was only a foot away from the huge pile that bounced up and down with every pot-hole we went over. This amused the driver who thought it very funny – at least it made him laugh. He was of course, immune, as he had long since become acclimatised to lorry loads of chillis.

The lorry did not have the problem of negotiating the hairpin bends as did the buses. It was shorter, and by taking a large sweep, could get around the bends without having to back, and so after an hour and a half Medan came into view spread out before us like a model town. In the distance, I could see what looked like a water tower, on top of which someone was walking around. Suddenly the figure toppled forward off the tower, followed by the noise of a machine gun; a plane shot overhead, banked no doubt to strafe anyone within range. My companion stopped the lorry and watched in horror. I could guess what he was thinking. We drove on and he took me straight to the airport where I got off, thanked the driver and wished him well.

I booked in and reported to Customs. As usual the Officer felt the four corners of the suitcase, but not the middle where my stamp album still lay covered in clothes. "Please take a seat," I was told. "The plane should be ready in two hours – the front seats have been removed to make way for additional fuel tanks and the pipe work is now being installed." I was too jittery to sit still. On the runway were the burnt-out remains of an aeroplane that had been shot up the day before by Japanese fighters. Occasionally I could hear the noise of heavy artillery and I began to wonder if I would ever get away. I walked up and down like a caged animal. Thoughts raced through my head. Perhaps the Japanese would arrive before we had taken off – would my parents and Jon be in Rangoon to meet me? I had still not received any definite news of them – would the plane be destroyed before we got away, like the burnt out wreck sitting at the end of a runway? – if my parents were not in Rangoon, what was I suppose to do? I had virtually no money and knew no one. I calmed myself down; of course, I would make my way to the offices of the Bombay Burma Trading Corporation, they would help me. The plane that was being modified was quite close to the terminal and, to my astonishment, on the nose was the name OEHOE, the very same plane that I flew in when it came down in the jungles of Siam.

When all was ready the passengers – and there were only a few – took their seats. The first seven rows of seats had been replaced with fuel tanks and pipes which led in all directions. I wondered if they knew what they were doing and hoped it would work. It became obvious to me that the question I had asked myself on the last occasion I was at the airport, had now been answered. These aeroplanes could not fly the distance from Medan to Rangoon without re-fuelling, and as this was no longer possible, because of the war, the only alternative was to carry extra fuel at the expense of passengers. Still, there were empty seats, which the stewardess who showed me to my seat explained was due to the weight of fuel, otherwise the plane would be too heavy to take off; as it was, it would slow our speed.

The Captain, whom I recognised, came to brief us. "We are attempting to fly to Rangoon as you all know, but there is considerable risk and we cannot be held responsible if we are shot down. You will have seen the burnt-out wreck of a plane on the runway; we are hoping to avoid detection but cannot be sure – anyway it is our only chance and it is most unlikely there will be any further aircraft landing at Medan before it falls to the the enemy. That is all for now, but we shall keep you informed of our progress." We took off. The Captain and co-pilot, whom I also recognised, both looked grim – not a smile, no time for pleasantries. Shortly after take off the co-pilot announced: "We have been spotted by a Japanese fighter that is after us. Please remain calm while we try to take evasive action." This consisted of banking the plane one way, then the other; presumably we would be more difficult to hit if the enemy were to open fire. I thought to myself that it would not be long before the fighter plane was in range as it must surely be faster than our heavily laden Dakota. Everyone was tense as we waited for trouble, but trouble never came.

Ten minutes later the co-pilot returned: "For reasons unknown to us the enemy aircraft has turned back and so for the moment we are clear to continue our journey to Rangoon." I looked out of the window, but all I could see was sea, not a sign of land anywhere. We none of us talked, the silence broken only by the radio operator over the noise of the engines. Four hours later the co-pilot returned. "I hope we are now out of trouble from enemy activity but we have to keep alert." He then returned to the cockpit. After six hours flying, the co-pilot re-appeared. "We have been diverted to Calcutta as the Japanese are getting near Rangoon." I had no idea of what I was to do in Calcutta, let alone whether there would be anyone there to meet me. The co-pilot continued: "Being diverted will add a further 670 miles to our journey, but with the additional fuel tanks we should have no difficulty in reaching Calcutta . In order to avoid enemy aircraft we have purposely being flying a westerly course which is all to the good." Some of the passengers started to talk among themselves; like me they were no doubt feeling more relaxed, though what I was to do in Calcutta still bothered me. We had been flying for ten hours when the co-pilot returned yet again: "We are commencing our descent to Dum Dum airport and hope to touch down in around fifteen minutes. We do apologise for asking you to retain your seat belts during the flight and that we have been unable to serve any food or drinks; getting clear of Medan was imperative and every minute counts. We also anticipated a certain amount of turbulence which you will have felt when we flew over the Andaman Islands and there was always the possibility of enemy aircraft. The Captain and his crew wish you all the best of luck for the future and hope that when the war is over we may have the pleasure of serving you again on KNILM Airways."

We landed ten minutes later. As I was leaving, the plane the pilot and co-pilot shook my hand, wished me well for the future and were only sorry that our acquaintance had to end in such a way, but at least we had all escaped being caught by the Japanese.

Sumatra fell sixteen days later to the Japanese on the 25th. February 1942. I had been lucky to get away.

Chapter 12

India

I was exhausted, but excited. The steps were wheeled out to the plane and we started to disembark. The sun was beginning to set, the heat of the day was over and it was pleasantly cool. At the bottom of the steps I stopped and looked toward the terminal. A group of people were waiting near the building; a man left the group and came toward me.

"I am Mr. Smith and I work for Wallace Brothers which is the holding company of your father's firm. You will be staying with me until we decide what we can best do for you."

"But, where are my parents and brother?" There was a long pause.

"Let us go to my car and perhaps I can explain on our journey home."

We got into the car; I had a dreadful sinking feeling in the pit of my stomach – something was wrong.

"I am most awfully sorry to say," Mr. Smith continued "we have no positive news from Bangkok apart from the fact that, like all the remaining British personnel, your mother, father and brother have been caught by the Japanese."

I was devastated. On reaching his house Mr. Smith took me into his study. "Please sit down" he said. "The news from Siam is very bad; we have good reason to believe that all British civilians have been executed and you will have to consider yourself an orphan. I know it will not be any consolation to you at present, but your father's company will look after you until you reach the age of 18 years."

I was used to hiding my feelings and did my best not to burst into tears, at least until I was alone.

Mr. Smith continued, "Living with me at present are 11 Quakers, all very kind, and members of the Friends Ambulance Unit – they drive ambulances on the Burma Road."

Master Patrick, Gibson
c/o Mr. Gibbons
11, Nepean Road,
Malabar Hill,
BOMBAY
c/o Mr J MB Gittons
or at Hallets School
Naini Tal
N. India

Tom Thompson,
Friends' Ambulance Unit,
B.R.C.S. 6133,
International Red Cross,
KWEIYANG,
Kweichow,
CHINA

公 誼 救 護 隊

FRIENDS' AMBULANCE UNIT : CHINA CONVOY
AFFILIATED TO THE INTERNATIONAL RELIEF COMMITTEE OF CHINA

TELEGRAMS:
INTREDCROSS KWEIYANGKWEI

KEWIYANG,
KWEICHOW.
27th. May 1942.

Refs.

Dear Pat,
      I was very pleased to receive your letter, that and one from my Father were the first letters I had. The Man who travelled across India with you (Christopher Sharman) should be in America by now..
      By now you have joined your school's Scout Troop I suppose. What are you? a P.L., or Second ?
      It's not very nice to say that you are having a rotten time with Mr.Gibbons, I'm sure he is trying to make things comfortable for you.
      We all got to Lashio safely after a very good trip by plane, the only one to feel sick was Reg Smith. Since then he and Sam Evans have been sent to work at the head office in Kweiyang, while I have been driving a truck (or lorry) up as far as Kunming and back again. I am in Kunming now and very soon I shall be going to the front to drive an ambulance. We have three doctors and eight other men to work in our mobile operating theatre.
      Seventeen of our men were working as ambulance drivers in Burma, and they are now in Calcutta, with another six men just sent out from England.
      Kunming is the best town I've been in so far but it is not so good as Calcutta. There are no trams taxis, very few buses, only one cinema, and it is not so clean as Calcutta. One town where I stayed for two weeks, Paoshan, is now just ruins from bombing.
      The rains have just started and they make the roads so slippery that unless we keep in the middle, we would slide off into a ditch. The last storm we had while I was coming here was so bad that we could not see properly and so we had to stop and wait until it finished.
      If I get any foreign stamps, I'll send them on to you.

Be good, and Keep Smiling,
Yours in Scouting,

P.S. I've forgotten your other name. Sorry Pat.

The Burma road was built between 1937 and 1939 as a supply route from China to the rest of the world. The Japanese had occupied the coastline cutting off all trade by sea. The Burma road stretched from Kunming in the province of Yunnan, to Lashio in Burma, a distance of six hundred and eighty one miles and until the Japanese overran Burma it was the only route in and out of China open to the sea.

I was taken to the lounge and introduced, shaking hands with each in turn. It was obvious that Mr. Smith had told them what to expect, but I think they were most surprised to find that I was not crying. They asked me where I had come from, whether I enjoyed school in Sumatra, and many other questions, but it was when I mentioned scouts that Tom Thompson became very interested. He had been a Troop Leader in England and wanted to hear about what I had done in Sumatra. I am sure Tom knew what was going on in my thoughts about being an orphan and helped me to get over my feelings of loneliness and distress. I became very attached to Tom and in the ensuing days he took me to see many places of interest in and around town, including the slum areas. After I left Calcutta we corresponded from time to time, which was kind of him as he must have been very busy. When his letters ceased, Dr. Edward Cadbury, a member of the Cadbury chocolate family, wrote to say that the vehicle that Tom and a colleague were driving had broken down somewhere on the Burma Road and that they had been attacked by bandits. During the struggle Tom almost lost his left forearm and was also badly cut on the other arm. However, he survived, thanks largely to the Sisters at Pichieh, run by German nuns and where he was able to convalesce.

My first night in India was Hell. As I lay in bed I could not think properly, I tried to visualise how my family had been put to death – had it been painful? I wept at the thought, wiped my eyes. What was I going to do now? More tears. Where was I to go? What family did I still have? ...thoughts came and went in a flash, I was confused. Then I remembered the last time I was in England, my school days at Uplands, holidays with my grandmother, I hated both and burst into tears again at the thought of it all. How long I remained like this I do not know, but eventually I fell asleep from exhaustion. I rose early in the morning and washed, determined that no one was to see that I had been crying.

I stayed in Calcutta for two weeks and during this time began to accept the fact that I was now orphaned. Perhaps it was because I had spent so much of my young life separated from the family that I got over the shock sooner than most. Mr. Smith had said that the Company would look after me until I was eighteen. Not that going to yet another school was anything but a bore. Now, if I could play games or take part in sports instead of going to lessons, that I would enjoy. My world had been turned upside down. I very much liked Mr. Smith and his Quaker friends, but inevitably, my stay in Calcutta soon came to an end. On the 23rd February, Christopher Sharman – who was also staying with Mr. Smith – and I, boarded the train for Bombay. We had a most comfortable compartment with an upper bunk, which I occupied, and a lower bunk, an adjoining toilet and wash basin. Our cases went underneath the lower bunk. The dining car was very Victorian with neat tables, little lights with cream-coloured shades were attached to each table and curtains hung at the windows, with pretty ornate rope sashes to hold them back unless the sun shone in brightly, when they could be released for protection from the glare. All the railway staff were in uniform.

The train did not break any speed records. I spent much of my time looking through the window at the countryside, a fascinating occupation: the varied vegetation, the people, housing, oxen, buffaloes harnessed to a wheel walking slowly and forever round in a circle drawing water from a well to irrigate the parched land; the meagre crops, the flies, the heat; the vendors, whenever we stopped at a station, selling papers, coconut, betel nut, tea, coffee, jelabies and other sweetmeats as they walked up and down the platform accosting anyone who looked out of a window or dared get out on to the platform. Prices were outrageous until you started to bargain when they quickly fell to a more acceptable level. I had learnt how to bargain years ago and with the aid of sign language managed to make myself understood. When in Calcutta I had acquired a penchant for jelabies which were very sweet and sticky.

After two days and a night we arrived at Bombay in the evening. I said goodbye to Christopher and wished him well on his journey to America. I was met by Mrs. Gibbons in a chaffeur-driven car and taken to her home on Malabar Hill. This is where the 'Burra Sahibs' live. Ornate wrought iron gates were opened to allow the car to proceed up the drive to the front door where servants waited instructions. It was a grand house. Mrs. Gibbons had red hair and it was obvious from the start that she did not like me and that the feeling was mutual.

Two weeks after my arrival Mrs. Gibbons took me to be 'fitted out' This meant all new clothes, shorts, shirts, underwear, additional clothing suitable for the foothills of the Himalaya mountains where I was to be sent to school. I saw very little of Mr. Gibbons who I presume was hectically busy at the office dealing with the many problems caused by the war. On my second day in Bombay, Mrs. Gibbons said,

"We are expecting a number of ships to arrive shortly, carrying refugees from Singapore, many are expected to be wounded and we have commandeered church halls and other large buildings as temporary housing so they can be cared for. We do need all the help we can get to assemble beds and to make them up, would you like to assist?"

"Yes," I said.

Soon we were taken to a large church hall where I was left, having first been been introduced to the person in charge. There were beds everywhere – the place was in chaos. I was introduced to another helper and we started to drag the beds into rows down both sides of the room. Then came the bed making. My partner and I were shown how to make a bed properly as it is done in hospital. We soon became very proficient and when one hall was ready we were moved to the next. By the end of the day, I was worn out and was grateful for a cool shower.

Fay

Fay Williams was on board one of the evacuee ships from Singapore that docked at Bombay. She had managed to get away but only just. Before the passengers were allowed to embark on the ship at Singapore they all had to sign a disclaimer that in the event of the ship being sunk, the Captain and crew were not to be held responsible. It was to be an old French vessel that was due for the scrap yard but, there was no option except to remain behind. In all, five ships set off from Singapore through the Malacca Straits in line astern, the first and last were sunk by Japanese bombers with the loss of all hands before reaching the Indian Ocean. The ship Fay was on could only manage five knots and broke down while still in the Malacca Straits and there she stayed for some days until the engineers were able to get the engines started again. The remaining two vessels continued full steam ahead until they were nearing Bombay when they too were caught by Japanese bombers and sunk with the loss of all hands. Fay was of the opinion that the only reason her ship was not bombed was that the Japanese believed it would sink before reaching its destination. It eventually took three weeks to reach Bombay but she did arrive to tell the tale.

Fay joined me at the Gibbons's house. Her parents had been next door neighbours of my family in Bangkok and her father also worked for the Bombay Burma Trading Corpoation. Fay and I met for the first time, she tells me, when we were three or four years old, in a cupboard in her parents' house in Bangkok. We neither of us had anything on. I don't remember any of this but have invariably found that a woman's memory for detail is far superior to a man's, so have to acknowledge that it is probably true.

At the time Fay had reached Bombay, her father was in hospital suffering from acute sciatica. He had been in Bombay helping in the building of ships when the Japanese declared war. His wife, Dorothy, was caught in Bangkok and was interned with my parents but Dorothy remained in the camp until released at the end of the war.

I was aware of the fact that my time in Bombay was strictly limited before I would be sent on my travels again, this time to a place called Naini Tal in the foothills of the Himalayas. What I did not know, until some fifty five years later, was that on my arrival in India, Mrs. Gibbons cabled my uncle in England, Humphrey Gibson, for instructions as to what was to be done with me. Should she try to get me on a troop ship back to England or was there anywhere else I should be sent? Humphrey cabled back saying that it would be most inadvisable for me to return to England in view of the war in Europe and suggested that, for the time being anyway, I should be sent to school in India. So the die was cast, I would be sent to the mountains where I would be out of the way.

I decided to make the most of my freedom while it lasted. I found Bombay too oppressive, with too many people, so spent most of my time at Breach Candy, a large well-appointed swimming pool. Here I could keep relatively cool and I soon made friends with three Tommies who were waiting to be posted to Calcutta and then on to the front line. We spent much of the time playing tag, and in the pool. Jock said

"Where do you live?"

"Malabar Hill," I replied.

"Gosh that's a posh area" said Jock,

"It is," said I. "But I don`t like it"

"Why don`t you like it?" said Fred

"Well I can`t explain, it`s just that I don`t fit in, they are all too posh for me, I feel as though I am intruding, which of course I am."

A moment later I dived in and heard a loud ping under the water; surfacing quickly I looked around expecting one of my friends to be after me, but they were still standing on the edge of the pool. It was then that I realised I had something sharp in my mouth. Taking it out, I discovered I had chipped a front tooth.

"Are you all right?" asked Andrew, "We thought you'd hit your head on the under-water vacuum cleaner."

"I hit a tooth, and here's the bit," I replied, as I threw the small fragment into some bushes.

That afternoon I returned to Malabar Hill for tea. Mrs. Gibbons noticed my tooth and said

"What on earth have you been doing to chip a tooth?"

"I was playing tag with three soldiers around the pool and in order to get away dived in without noticing the under water vacuum cleaner. Unfortunately I hit my tooth and chipped it."

"Are they nice soldiers?" asked Mrs. Gibbons.

"Very nice," I said.

"Well why not ask them to tea tomorrow afternoon?"

"That would be lovely, I will.Thank you very much," I replied.

The very next day I saw my three friends as usual and invited them for tea. Jock who was always the more talkative said,

"Are you quite sure she wants us for tea? The three of us have been in Bombay for a month and so far you're the only civilian who has ever spoken to us let alone invited us into their home."

"Yes, I'm quite sure," I replied.

So the afternoon saw us strolling up the drive toward the house when Mrs. Gibbons appeared at the front door and beckoned to me. The three soldiers paused and I went to see what she wanted.

"Are those your friends?" said Mrs. Gibbons.

"Yes," I replied.

"But they are non-commissioned officers and I will not have any soldier in my house below the rank of Captain."

"But," I stuttered, "What am I to tell them. You suggested they came to tea. I can't tell them to go away."

"You'll have to."

And at that Mrs. Gibbons went in and shut the door. I felt deeply embarrassed as I walked back to my friends. Luckily they had guessed what had happened. Jock said, "We thought your invitation was too good to be true, but don't worry, we'll treat you to tea in a little cafe near our barracks."

During my stay in Bombay I saw little of Fay except for meals. She was to go to a convent school in Ootacamund in the Nilgiri Hills, 485 miles south of Bombay whilst I would be going 850 miles north of Bombay to the Himalayas.

One day Fay said, "I'm going to visit my father in hospital, would you like to come with me?"

"Yes, very much." I replied.

So we caught a bus and half an hour later arrived at the hospital. Mr. Williams, when we saw him, was lying in bed on the verandah shaded from the sun by a red and blue coloured awning. There was a gentle breeze which cooled the heat from the afternoon sun. At first Fay's father did not appear to see us; perspiration was running down his face and his pyjama top was soaked. Suddenly he realised it was Fay; I am not sure if he recognised me, probably not, but he was furious. "Get out," he shouted wincing with pain. "I don't want to see anyone." A nurse appeared as if from nowhere and took us aside. "Mr. Williams," she said "is in a lot of pain, he can't sleep and dare not move. The pain killers we have given him have not helped his sciatica and he doesn't want to see anybody, please go home." Fay, not surprisingly, was visibly upset and close to tears. Nurse said, "We'll phone you when he is in less pain so that you can visit again."

It was the last time I saw Mr. Williams. A few days later I was on the train to Naini Tal. Mr. Williams did recover and at the end of the war he and his wife, who had survived internment, settled down in South Africa.

And so my stay in Bombay was coming to a close. I bade farewell to my three friends at Breach Candy which saddened me as we had had a lot of fun together. The day arrived for me to leave. I must have appeared rather forlorn and I certainly felt miserable as Fay said, "Cheer up dear old Pat, I'm sure school won't be half as bad as you expect. When I get to Ooty I'll write to you and I'll expect you to write to me, so don't forget." Fay is one of those people who is always cheerful and full of life, a great companion.

P.S. Daddy has just had a telegram from London saying that both your parents o Mummy are well.

NAZARETH CONVENT HIGH SCHOOL,
OOTACAMUND.

P.P.S. I have played a game June 8th of Ping Pong too, and I will try & get more practice, then we can play in the holidays. (F.W).

Dear old Pat,
How are you getting on at school? I hope you got my last letter alright, but I would'nt be at all surprised if you have'nt, because for the life of me I can't remember posting it. However this one ought to reach you alright.

The school up here is awfully nice. It is situated overlooking the lake, and we have a beautiful view of the whole of Ooty from here. The girls here are all jolly nice especially to new girls. I thought it would be awful at first. Every-morning before breakfast we have games, usually tennis, net ball or cricket.

I have been collecting more stamps recently. Three other girls up here collect them, and I have been given quite a few and swapped quite a few.

There is the sweetest dog from the farm which often comes & pays us a visit during class, & they have decided to have it put to sleep.

2/
NAZARETH CONVENT HIGH SCHOOL,
OOTACAMUND.

It has just had the most adorable pups, and they have got to be drowned too. Everyone is frightfully sorry.

There are quite a few other schools up here & they are all taking Junior & Senior Cambridge. I have got to take my Junior too at the end of the year, so I will be staying on a bit later on the end of the term. However I am going to ask Daddy if I can stay on the other end to make up for it.

Yesterday I had to come to the infirmary for a period of three days, because I got a slight chill as well as a cough and cold. It is the most awful nuisance as I am missing the weekend, and just get up in time for the work on the Monday. The exams are starting next week and we are made to work, work, work!!!

The other day during the holidays we were allowed to go and watch the races. It was rather good fun. We backed Julie's of horses, and they invariably won.

Well Pat old thing, I will end now, but please write soon, a nice long letter please, & then I will write again.

Tons of love from
Fay

Chapter 13

Journey to Naini Tal

It was mid March 1942 that I was to start my journey to Naini Tal. Before going to the station Mrs. Gibbons asked me to go into the lounge.
"Your trunk, with all your clothes have been sent on ahead and will be at the school when you arrive. I have arranged for you to stay at a boarding house during the holidays where I am sure you will be happy. I hope you have a good journey and that you enjoy Naini Tal. Good-bye and take care of yourself."

"Thank you for looking after me while I've been in Bombay and please thank Mr. Gibbons too." I replied. In fact I was not to leave the foothills of the Himalayas for the next twenty six months.

At that Mrs. Gibbons gave a peremptory wave of her hand, and left the room. I had the feeling that she was only too glad to see the back of me, however the feeling was mutual. Before leaving I said goodbye to all the servants I could find; they had always been friendly toward me, though I felt that Mrs. Gibbons disapproved. I got into the waiting car clutching my suitcase, and listened while the tyres crunched the gravel beneath them as we went around the semicircular drive and on to the road. This, I reflected was the end of another period in my life and wondered if I would ever be back again. I had enjoyed swimming at Breach Candy and talking to Fay about the past and the future. What was in store for me in Naini Tal was anyone's guess. Yet again I was off to a place I had never been to before and knew no one. I had a sinking feeling in the pit of my stomach, a feeling that had become commonplace since the Japanese entered the war, a feeling of uncertainty, when would it all end? I could not see into the future and what little I could see I did not like.

The chauffeur drove me to the railway station where I said goodbye to him – the only person to see me off, in his immaculate suit and peaked cap, and I then boarded the train that I hoped would eventually take me to Kathgodam which is the nearest station to Naini Tal. Placing my KLM suitcase on the rack above the bench seat I looked around the compartment. Apart from myself it was empty; the upholstery, which had been red, was now a dirty brown and badly worn. It reminded me of British rolling stock but of a great age, probably pre the first World War. The train belonged to The Bombay Baroda and Central India line, nothing like as comfortable as on my journey from Calcutta to Bombay, and not air-conditioned, which meant that the windows had to be open in order to get away from the relentless heat, as the train chugged slowly northwards. The open windows allowed soot from the steam engine to blow in so it was soon possible to write my name in dust and grime on the mirrors either side of the compartment, but at least it was cool.

The train was travelling up the coast so from time to time I could see the sea and green vegetation. Visiting the dining car I looked at the menu for dinner, but nothing on offer whetted my appetite so I returned to my compartment. We stopped at many minor stations until we reached Baroda where there was a wait for an hour. I got out to stretch my legs and to buy some sandwiches and a drink. I glanced at the paper stand but it seemed that all the papers were in an Indian language probably Urdu or Hindi. Walking along the platform I was assailed by little children and tradesmen plying their ware, but shook my hand to indicate I was not interested. Railway engines have always fascinated me so I took a look at the engine pulling my train and others besides. All the rolling stock looked old but at least it worked.

I returned to my train and having eaten my sandwiches decided to settle down for the night as it was now dark. I raised the windows, leaving a small gap at the top to allow for air and then pulled down the blinds. I locked both doors and stretched out along the bench seat and made myself as comfortable as possible using my jacket as a pillow.

By now we had left the coast and were travelling northeast to Godhra, Kota and on to Muttra with the usual number of intermediate stops in between. Whenever the train came to a halt there was the sound of voices as people walked up and down the platform selling their wares. The heat in the compartment was oppressive and it was difficult to get any sleep.

It was midday when we reached Muttra (Mathura) and here I had to change and wait for another train. Muttra is said to be the dustiest town in the world and in my opinion it lived up to its reputation. As I stepped out of the carriage, topee on and carrying my suitcase, I noticed groups of maimed bodies lining the platform. Some had one leg, one had no legs, there were still more with arms, hands or feet missing and so it went on. Faces full of scars from smallpox, it was a truly horrifying sight. Despite their terrible handicaps they all seemed able to move with surprising speed. At one end of the platform, was what I assumed to be a dead body, rolled up in a blanket. I was the only European to alight at Muttra and before I realised what was happening, I was surrounded by beggars: 'No Mama, no Papa, buckshees munkta'.... came the cry from all around. I was terrified. The man nearest to me had one leg and only one eye, flies covered his face and in particular the eye socket which was suppurating. He was much more agile with his makeshift, bent wooden crutch and one leg than most of the others. Children with protruding ribs and pot bellies, some deformed, pulled at my clothing and looked up at me piteously with their hands outstretched for money. A mother with leg sores, covered in flies, and with only one hand, a child at her breast, supported by her handless arm while she held out a begging bowl with the only hand she possessed. The baby was a mere skeleton and I was amazed it was even alive. The mother had no milk to give it. Fortunately for me I was rescued by the Station Master. At his command the crowd dispersed, once more to return to their allotted place on the platform to await the next train of unsuspecting passengers. I had been told that life expectancy in India was thirty-seven years, but for these poor souls it must have been far less.

I asked my saviour, "When is the train due in for Bareilly?"

"Perhaps in three hours or maybe six, it all depends," was his reply.

"What does it depend on?" I asked.

"Anything could happen, we did not see a single train for three days a short time ago," was his reply.

"When do you expect the next train for Bareilly, assuming it arrives on time?" I asked.

"In about three hours time, all being well."

A goods train chugged slowly through the station; there was a rustle of maimed bodies, but at the Station Master's command nobody moved from their allotted spot; the train did not stop. At this point I gave up the conversation and decided to look around town; at least I would be away from the station.

The town, or what little I saw of it, was very dirty and a strong breeze blew rubbish and dust around everywhere. Wherever I went I was the centre of attraction and people stared at me. They had probably never seen an European. An old man approached me. He was wearing a filthy dhoti, but his lined and weather-beaten face had an air of resignation and authority.

" Please, Sahib, don`t go any further, there is a cholera epidemic here at present and many people have died."

"Thank you for warning me," I said.

So I turned around and started back to where I had come from. On approaching the station I was concerned that I would be accosted again by those poor disfigured people waiting for the next train, but was relieved to find a roadside entrance to a waiting room unheeded by those on the platform. It was very dirty. Spittoons were arranged around the walls but as much betel nut had hit the walls as had gone into the receptacles. I remained in solitary confinement for over four hours, the boredom relieved by the occasional walk along a dust track that ran from the back of the station and parallel to the railway line. Sometimes, I met a bullock cart going in the opposite direction, usually driven by a woman and with a group of half starved children. As always I was the centre of attraction. I never ventured further than a couple of hundred yards from the station in case my train should arrive.

At last another passenger train drew in, the Station Master went up and down the platform, shouting, "This train is for Bareilly calling at Hathras, Kasganj, Budaun,.........." and so on. Thank God, I thought, this is my train. I pulled open the waiting room door and made a mad dash into the nearest carriage. Half an hour later the train pulled out on its way to Bareilly. By this time I was both hungry and very thirsty so at the next stop I made my way to the dining car. Dinner of a hot Madras curry, rice and chapati together with innumerable cups of tea revived my spirits. That night I slept better and when I woke up in the morning we had already arrived at Bareilly. The last sixty five miles or so saw me having breakfast as the train wound its way wearily toward the foothills of the Himalayas.

We arrived at Kathgodam mid morning where I alighted and caught the bus to Naini Tal. In some ways, the scenery, as we climbed zigzagging ever higher, reminded me of the road to Kaban Djahe without the overhanging hairpin bends. Langur monkeys rushed here and there swinging from tree to tree. Brightly coloured parakeets were everywhere and small vivid blue birds, which I assumed to be kingfishers, darted in and out of the trees; but they were so quick that it was difficult to be sure. Occasionally I got a glimpse of beautifully coloured butterflies but was never able to get a proper look at them. The scenery was spectacular the higher we went. Rhododendrons and magnolia were in bloom, very tall and stately in all their finery. When there was a gap in the trees I could see for miles down in the plains, which I had only recently left behind. It was as though I was in an aeroplane slowly getting higher with every break in the vegetation as I looked down on the world below.

At last we arrived at the bus station at one end of the lake which is Naini Tal. (Tal means lake). This was the end of the road and everyone got off the bus. Naini Tal lies in the Kumaon district of the Himalayas, an area that has become well known through the books of Jim Corbett, the great conservator and hunter. He lived at Gurney House, which still stands not far from the lake. Naini lies in a bowl surrounded by mountains. Opposite Beetle Hill, where stood the Hallett War School, is Mount Ayarpetta, and Sherwood College, which had a reputation for excellence. Not far from Sherwood College a path led to Dorothy's Seat, put there by an Englishman in memory of his wife.

The town is situated around the side of the lake, which is about one mile long and five hundred and fifty yards wide and is surrounded by seven peaks, the highest of which, Mount Cheena, rises, two thousand two hundred feet from the lake. The Hallett War School, where I was to go, was on Beetle Hill some nine hundred feet above the town. I asked someone in the bus station to direct me to the school and was told to ask a dandy wallah to take me there. A dandy is a chair for one, slung between two poles carried by two men one in front and the other behind. The men carrying me were very lithe and climbed the hill at a steady trot. On the way I noticed the games fields and various buildings all on different levels. I alighted outside the office, gave the bearers each a few annas, and went in.

Chapter 14

Hallett War School

On my arrival I was shown to the Headmaster's Office where I met the Reverend Robert C. Llewelyn. He was tall, well built, with aquiline features, and dark hair, a centre parting and a beak-like nose. It was also quite apparent that he was covered in dark hair as it could be seen through his shirt. He stood up and we shook hands. He then sat down again.

"I am the Headmaster: this school was opened in January last year and we took it over from Philander Smith College. At the time the college was instructed to leave as the authorities believed the hillside might slip into the lake. However, later calculations on the movement of the ground re-assured the governing body that there was no likelihood of this happening in the foreseeable future. By this time Philander Smith College had found other premises, so it was decided that we would take over the school, which was then named after Lady Hallett, wife of the Governor of the Upper Province of India. The main purpose of the school is to continue the education of boys and girls whose fathers are fighting the Japanese. As you will have been told by Mrs. Gibbons term has already started. Any questions?"

"No," I said.

"If you behave and work diligently you have nothing to fear. I will call Matron and ask her to take you to your dormitory."

A few minutes later Matron came in: The dormitory was at the highest point of the school and my bed was in the middle, on the opposite side to the windows. The back of the building, which had no windows, overlooked a cemetery 1,000 feet below, in the front a parade ground where PE was held before breakfast. Matron said, "The pupils will finish class in a few minutes so you will have company."

A short while later some of the boys entered and I introduced myself. They were all very friendly. Michael Rose said,

"Come on, I will show you Snow View, it`s a wonderful sight."

We set off along a path and before long came to an opening in the hill from where we could see the snow capped peaks of the mountains.

"That's Nanda Devi, over 25,600 feet and the fifth highest peak in the world." All I could make out was a lot of low-lying cloud.

"I can't see any mountains, only clouds in the distance." I answered.

"Those aren't clouds, you idiot, they're mountains."

I had made the same mistake as many before me have made when seeing for the first time the great chain that are the Himalayas.

I usually manage to get along with most people and the Hallett War School was no exception. I joined the school Scout Troop and because I had already obtained quite a number of badges was soon made Patrol leader of the Wolf Patrol. I am afraid the enthusiasm for scouting in the school was not comparable to what it had been in Kaban Djahe. I enjoyed playing football and also hockey, which is an Indian tradition, but, as usual, found myself as goal keeper due to my inability to run without getting asthma.

A game we often played was Gillie Dunda. This consisted of a small piece of wood about four to six inches long and an inch in diameter sharpened to a point at both ends, and a rough wooden club. The idea was to strike the piece of wood at one end with the club and as it flew upwards hit it as far as possible. The club was then placed on the ground in front of the striker. Whoever retrieved the piece of wood would throw it to see if they could hit the club on the ground. If successful the striker and retriever would exchange places. The striker could also be caught out. Runs can be scored by pacing out the distance between the striker and where the piece of wood came to rest.

Unfortunately, I could not concentrate on the lessons which meant I came bottom in most subjects except mathematics and overall I was almost always bottom of the class. This situation came to a head early on when I was summoned to see the Headmaster.

"Your weekly report says that you do not pay attention and are not trying, what have you to say for yourself?" said the Rev.Llewelyn.

"I am sorry, Sir, but I cannot concentrate," I replied.

Patrol leaders, Hallett War School 1942

"Well, I will help you to concentrate! Pull down your trousers and pants and bend over that chair, I am going to give you four of the best."

And so began the first of many beatings, usually at 4.30 pm. on a Saturday afternoon. The caning left large weals accross my backside and for the next day it felt tender when I sat down. Unfortunately, it made no impression on my work as I still continued to come bottom of the class, resulting in the Saturday afternoon appointments.

The subject that I dreaded most was English. Mrs. Austin taught English and for homework she frequently set the class an essay to write. At this I was utterly useless. Each pupil would have to read out their essay which would then be criticised by her and by other pupils. When it came to my essay everyone was in hysterics, except Mrs Austin, who went red in the face to match her red hair. She was of course perfectly right; my essays were dreadful. Eventually the day came when Mrs Austin read out all the essays one after another leaving mine until last. When she had read this aloud there was the usual laughter but, to my great surprise, she turned on the class and said, "If you think that Gibson's essay is bad, which it is, the rest of them are even worse." You could have heard a pin drop. From that moment my essays were not always the worst.

Canings continued; sometimes it was the whole dormitory who would line up to be caned one after another, always for some trivial offence where the culprit would not own up. On one occasion Paul was caught twiddling his toes at the end of the bed after lights were out at 9 o'clock and was caned, but not before he had to be held down by two prefects. As was the custom with the Rev. Llewelyn, he held out his hand to shake after the caning, but Paul, who was an excellent pugilist simply smacked it away and challenged him to a boxing match. The Rev. Llewelyn surprisingly accepted. So a few days later they met in the ring. The match lasted less than two rounds with the Rev. Llewelyn receiving a bloody nose and a very swollen eye; he had to throw in the towel to cheers from all the boys.

What turned out to be one of my biggest mistakes soon after arriving at the Hallett War School, was my first meeting with Mrs. Fisher. She said to me,

"Gibson, can you sing?"

"I was in the choir in my last school," I replied.

"Good," said Mrs. Fisher. "We have choir practice every week and I would like you to attend."

There was not only the practice, but I was expected to sing in Chapel every Sunday at every service. Unfortunately, being obliged to attend so many services not only annoyed me intensely, but set me against religion for years to come.

It was during my first full term at the Hallett that the monsoon started and the rain poured down accompanied by much thunder and lightning. A group of boys and I were watching the fireworks from the safety of the dormitory when lightning struck the cables supplying electricity to the building. It bounced along the wires, in what looked like slow motion, until it reached the dormitory when there was a loud bang; all the light bulbs blew and we were showered with tiny fragments of glass.

I had not long been at Naini Tal when it became apparent that the height of 7,500 feet was affecting my health, as I constantly had an upset stomach and was losing weight. Miss Lowe, the Matron of the

Senior Boys, noticed I was getting thinner and told me to take Radio Malt, which I liked, after every meal. This stabilised my weight at 6 stone, but even when I eventually left Naini Tal at the age of fifteen years, I still weighed exactly 6 stone. Although Naini was not particularly high, it is a fact that some people are affected by height, especially if they remain well above sea level for a long time. Another boy became so ill at this altitude that he had to return to the plains.

The dormitory that I was in had a large bathroom at one end of the building. Galvanised baths were filled the previous night with cold water and every boy had to take a cold bath in the morning, on an in and out basis, that was supervised by the prefects to ensure that all boys took their turn. On jumping out of the bath we towelled down and put on our PE clothes, then paraded on the forecourt in front of the building. These cold baths were bearable during the summer months, but when winter arrived it was sometimes necessary for the prefects to break the ice on the surface before we could get in and that really was an ordeal.

Rabies

In August 1942 I awoke in the early hours of the morning to find that, try as I might, I could not stretch my legs to the bottom of the bed. It was very dark so it was not possible to see what was there. Pushing back the bedclothes, I gave a hard kick. Something gave my ankle a nip, followed by a dull thump and whatever it was fell on the floor. I pulled up the blankets, turned over and went back to sleep.

The following morning a dead dog was found near the front door of the building. Despite enquiries nobody knew anything about the poor animal, but its death was confirmed as probably being due to rabies. The dormitory was lined up as usual early one morning but before commencing PE, the House Master wanted to know who, if anyone, had touched the dog. A few boys thought they might have touched the dog at some time and put up their hands. I told of my encounter with an unknown object the night before the dog was found. We were all to have anti-rabies injections, I and possibly one other boy would be given fourteen injections, one each day for fourteen days and the other boys only seven injections.

Before the course of treatment started, each of us was interviewed. Details of our parents, their addresses and other information was asked for. The treatment was to be carried out by the school doctor Major I.M.S. Holines who lived on Beetle Hill but a little lower down nearer the lake. The arrangements finalised we arrived at the surgery and took our turn for the injection. I was one of the last to go, but felt reassured as the boys had felt nothing. My turn arrived.

"What is your name?" said Major Holines.

"Gibson," I replied.

Turning to his nurse he said, "No anaesthetic for this patient, his father is a civilian." I did not at first appreciate the significance of this remark. "Lie on the bed, pull up your shirt and vest and loosen your trousers, I am going to give you an injection in the stomach. After the first injection I shall leave the needle in your stomach while I refill the syringe so I don't want you to move."

I did as I was told. When I saw the syringe I was shocked by the size; it was enormous. The needle went in, I gasped with pain, it took at least a minute to empty the syringe, there was then a pause while the needle was left in my stomach and the syringe refilled for the second time. When it was all over there was a lump the size of a tennis ball. The doctor massaged the lump to help disperse the swelling.

"Did the other boys have an anaesthetic before the main injection?" I asked.

"Yes," he replied

"Why can't I have one too?" I said.

"My instructions are that only families who are members of the Armed Forces are to have an anaesthetic and your father was a civilian," he replied.

And so I dreaded the following thirteen days. Even now I cannot comprehend why any child should be put through this torture because his parent was not in uniform fighting at the front.

My memories of Naini Tal were not so much of my school-days, but of the holidays. I was troubled by my thoughts. How had my parents and brother died? What was to happen to me when I left Naini? Would I remain in India or be sent somewhere else in the world? Past and future were all jumbled up in my mind, making it impossible to learn. Anyway, I hated my lessons and longed to be on my own and I could only be alone when on holiday. I paid little or no attention in class and wasted the two years I was there. It was no

The Hallett War School 1943

fault of the teachers; many of the pupils did very well academically. Most of the staff were women who found it difficult to keep order in class, except Mrs Austin.

One morning, during a Maths lesson, I was distracted by a centipede crawling up my arm. It was about nine inches long and gave me a fright. Although they are harmless, if frightened, they can dig their legs into flesh and then cannot get them out, so their bodies wriggle, but they are unable to move backwards or forwards. The only way to deal with this situation if it arises, is to burn them off, leaving a life-long scar where the legs had been. So to prevent this happening, I had been told either to flick it off or to knock it hard in the direction it was crawling. I flicked and the centipede landed on the floor. I took my penknife from my pocket, opened the blade and threw it at the centipede, cutting it in two. The blade stuck in the wooden floor. Retrieving my knife I threw it again cutting more off the centipede and so I continued until a voice said,

"Gibson what are you doing?"

"Killing a centipede that was on my arm," I replied.

"Put the knife away and if I ever catch you playing with it again during my lesson I shall report you to Rev. Llewelyn," said Mrs. Ruffell.

Me in Naini Tal 1943

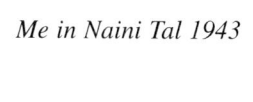

Me and Jimmy Pointon, Naini Tal

Chapter 15

The Forest

I was fascinated by the forest. There was something about it that caught my imagination – it was exciting, always interesting and on every visit there would be something new to find: the poisonous quill of a porcupine, the newly shed skin of a snake, the pug marks of many different animals which I could not identify and many ants, which were best avoided as their bite produced red weals on my skin. Consequently, during the school holidays I would visit the forest around Naini as often as I could, walking alone with my thoughts. Here I felt at home, I could relax, but at the same time be on my guard. I enjoyed tracking the deer through the dense undergrowth of bracken, keeping down-wind so that they would not smell my scent, and a feeling of satisfaction would come over me when I managed to get close enough to watch their twitching noses, their ears turning this way and that to pick up any sounds that could spell danger.

Nobody ever asked me what I was doing or where I was going. As I had a good appetite someone might have wondered what had happened if I had failed to appear at meal times. A city dweller would soon get lost among the trees in a forest, especially if he had no compass, just as I was lost when I returned to London, not being used to seeing so many buildings.

When I left Naini or the school grounds there were always certain precautions that had to be taken to avoid trouble. There were two main hazards. The first were the monkeys who carried rabies, so I used to go armed with a stout staff for protection when walking in the forest. The other problem was scorpions, whose sting can be lethal. Before sitting on a stone I learned always to turn it over because there was usually a scorpion under it. Never put on shoes until the heel had been banged hard on the ground to knock out any scorpion that might be sheltering there. It took me two years to get over this habit once I had returned to Britain. Leeches were also plentiful and I often found them clinging to my legs when walking in the forest. It was easy for me to tell when they were sucking my blood due to the irritation they caused. As a precaution I always carried a small bag of salt which I applied to any leech misguided enough to attach itself to my legs. On application of the salt they very quickly dropped off.

Black Panthers were in the forest but I only ever saw one and it gave me an awful fright. Jimmy Pointon with her dog, which was ahead of us, and I were walking along 'Panther Path' as it was known, and ran along the edge of the forest on the south side of the lake, towards Dorothy's Seat. Suddenly, a black shape leapt from the bough of a tree, grabbed the dog by the neck and in a few bounds was high in the branches of another tree; I suspect the dog had been killed by the very first bite. Jimmy Pointon screamed and I froze; it all happened in a matter of seconds.

Mountain bears frequented the forest but kept well away from man. The occasional rogue tiger, driven from the forest lower down, due to old age or some injury that prevented it from hunting, found its food by preying on domestic animals further up the mountains. When this happened, the villagers would get together, track and kill the tiger. What I saw most often were deers, the small Kakkar and the much larger Ghoral. Their brown-grey colouring made them difficult to see in the bracken-covered undergrowth.

Gradually I became accustomed to the nature and feeling of the forest and had no difficulty in finding my way around. The angle of a hillside in the distance, a particular tree, a landslide, an outcrop of rock, small streams, all became landmarks so that I knew exactly where I was at any time. Then there were the signs of the inhabitants of the forest, animal droppings, pug marks, twigs recently broken, bits of fur caught on bushes where an animal had rushed passed. I came to recognise the grunt of a wild boar which was too close for comfort; Langur monkeys quarrelling in the treetops. Where the sun managed to shine through the canopy of intertwining leaves, there were the occasional exotic, multi-coloured birds to be seen such as jungle fowl, minivets, white-eye minahs, hill minahs and the hoopoe, but these sightings were rare. The forest of oak, rhododendrons, spruce, cypress and deodar, a world of shadows, high in the trees a kind of green opalescence; lower down a misty grey and on the ground dark impenetrable blackness below which lived another form of life: snakes, (which were reputed to be non-poisonous), stag and cow beetles often two to three inches long. The male beetles have very long jointed jaws which are branched like the antlers of a stag, hence the name. At school we would place two stag beetles in a kind of dust bowl along with a cow beetle. The two stags would usually fight over the cow. The ensuing battle was interesting to watch as they wrestled with each other and we took bets on the winner. The two stags would use their antlers and the winner was invariably the beetle able to get his antlers directly between the head and thorax of his opponent and then squeeze, thus pulling off his opponent's head.

There were centipedes a foot long, armies of ants, scorpions, porcupines three feet long with sharp pointed quills, frogs and many other small animals that scuttled to and fro. I wore no boots, only metal-studded chuplis, a kind of sandal, which I often had to have re-studded in the bazaar, and as I frequently ran up and down through the bracken I needed to be aware of everything that was going on underfoot.

Along the track that led from Naini to Bhimtal where I had to scramble over rocks, the going was steep; then suddenly I would find myself looking down on Bhimtal where people looked like ants and bullocks like black beetles moving slowly about. The lake was a mirror reflecting the sun's rays. As I continued down, people and animals gradually assumed their right proportions. By the time I had reached Bhimtal the ground had levelled off. The area around the lake was being farmed. The natives were poor, scratching a living from the earth; their bullocks were like skeletons. I remember on one occasion watching the impending death of a bullock. The animal could hardly keep upright; it staggered around; Lammergeyer vultures, the largest bird of prey in the world with a wing span of nearly ten feet when fully grown, circled overhead; they knew what was going to happen. At last the poor creature collapsed. The vultures came in for the kill, first pecking out its eyes, then going for the belly and within minutes the entrails were strewn over the ground, each vulture vying with its neighbour for the juiciest bit. It made me feel sick to watch. (It was a Lammergeyer vulture that took the stop netting from one of the goals on the football pitch at the Hallett War School, for its nest.)

During this particular visit to Bhimtal I was caught in a storm. It was the time of the monsoon and the rain fell in sheets with such force that a vulture, flying above me, was driven into the tree I was beneath. It crashed through many branches until finally finding a foothold on which to fold its wings and compose itself. I used to carry a catapult made from a stout Y-shaped branch of tree and a good elastic which was cut from the cross section of a tyre inner tube, with a piece of soft leather three inches long and an inch wide to hold the stones I used. Two slots were made in the leather, one at each end and the elastic fed in one slot and out of the other; this held the leather in place. In my pockets were many round stones. The vulture was about twenty five feet above me and I could clearly see the underside of its body. I don't think it was aware of my presence but, even if it had been, there was little it could do about it under the present circumstances. The opportunity was too good to miss. Selecting a round stone I fitted it into the leather; taking careful aim, I pulled back the elastic as far as I could and let go. The stone flew upwards with considerable force and hit the vulture, which, whether due to shock or pain, shot out of the tree and was then battered to the ground by the rain. I selected another stone, but by this time the vulture had seen me and decided to run for protection beneath other nearby trees where it was able to fly upwards into the branches that were protecting it from the rain.

Walking to Bhimtal, five miles south east of Naini, took two hours but the return journey, uphill all the way, took twice as long and the path eventually emerged near Snow View where there is a wonderful spot for picnics called Lyria Canta. This is probably the most wonderful view anywhere in Naini Tal. On a clear day I could marvel at the beauty of the line of mountains known to all as the Himalayas with Nandi Devi seventy miles to the north. On a clear night, looking south towards the plains, the lights of Bareilly could be seen eighty miles away. Fortunately for me, the unpolluted air suited my asthma, for I only had two attacks in the twenty six months I was there. When I first arrived, I found that I quickly got out of breath because of the altitude. However, my lungs gradually expanded to cope with the rarefied conditions. I always felt that there were higher schools in other parts of India and in the Andes, but was assured that the Hallett was the highest school in the world.

Mount Cheena

Naini Tal is a very beautiful hill station. The north end is called Mallital and its southern end Tallital. The bus that takes people from the railway station of Kathgodam to Naini Tal terminates at the southern end of the lake where there is also a bazaar. Naini is surrounded on all sides by mountains. There are frequent minor landslides and the inhabitants soon get used to the rumble of stones as they cascade down the escarpments. In winter when the snow piles up on the slopes, minor avalanches occur daily. The shafts of sunlight shining through the tumbling snow spray gives a rainbow effect which, set against the background of the sheer cliff face, produces a remarkable colour combination.

These are old fold mountains consisting mainly of slate which is inclined to come away in sheets as you walk and because the edges are so sharp shoes very soon wear out. In September 1880 there was a dreadful tragedy when five hundred feet came off the top of Mount Cheena, filling in half a mile of lake and burying almost all the inhabitants. It is still the highest of the seven peaks which comprise Naini Tal, rising two thousand two hundred feet above the lake, and looking at it from below, there is a sheer drop of about one thousand feet before the ground starts to level off.

All the seven mountains that surround the lake have footpaths to the top. To climb up and down all of them in one day is quite a feat. The paths are very stony and with every step forward you can slip two steps back if you are not careful. Providing you keep to the paths the walks are quite safe and if you were not sufficiently energetic to walk, it was possible to hire a donkey from the lakeside which, for a few annas, would carry you up to the top. There was one dangerous spot for anyone with no head for heights. On the far side of Cheena, which cannot be seen from the lake, there had been another landslide. The slope is not sheer but very steep. The path crossed the slide but is only about two feet wide. Looking down the slide it disappeared into the forest about three to four hundred feet below. To slip could be fatal. In the summer holidays I would sometimes take a party of visitors up Cheena until, on one occasion, I had a very worrying experience. When crossing the landslide I always insisted that only one person crossed at a time, without looking down: the distance was about forty feet to the other side. Anyone who was frightened stayed behind. On this particular day, in June 1943, a middle aged gentleman walked halfway across, looked down and was so frightened he could not move or speak, he just shook. Everyone watched. I did not have any idea of what to do. Fortunately a charcoal burner, (a native who collects wood and turns it into charcoal for cooking), noticed the man trembling and without putting down his bundle of sticks, which were twice his height, walked up to the man, took him by the hand and led him back across the slide. The man was ashen and perspiration was pouring down his face. After this experience I only took commandos who were there to train how to scale a vertical rock face.

How I became involved with the commandos will always remain a mystery. The stocky Scottish colonel who approached me in the first place, simply said he had been told that I was the only English-speaking guide in the area. Although I knew the region well I had never thought of myself as a guide. However, always willing to earn a few rupees I took on the job, never realising how tough he and his men were. The Colonel looked up at Mount Cheena and said

"That will do for a start."

"When do you want to leave?" I replied.

"Now," said he.

He was commanding a platoon of about twenty men, dressed in full battle gear. I was very lightly dressed. We commenced at a brisk pace along one of the many footpaths that ended at the top. There was no stopping on the way to get one's breath and the only person glad to sit down when we finally reached the summit was me. All the way the Colonel never stopped asking me questions on what I was doing in Naini and about my life in general. The men started their training immediately under the instructions of the Colonel, who was quite obviously highly respected. Somebody had also told the Colonel about the seven peaks that surround Naini and that to climb them all in a day was considered a feat. The next day I was instructed to be ready to move off at sunrise, the men would carry lunch for us all. We set off at a steady three miles per hour which I found hard going on the uneven terrain. Until I had got my second wind I trailed behind rather than leading the platoon. I have always found it necessary to start exercising slowly, otherwise I become breathless and can't continue. The men were again in full battle gear and as the day got warmer perspiration poured down their faces and their shirts became damp with sweat. There was no stopping. We drank as we climbed up and down the hills, in the meanwhile the Colonel continued to ask me questions. The seven peaks were not really a climb, more an endurance test. We completed the climb in time for a late lunch on the top of the seventh peak, and an excellent lunch it was. The men were allowed to rest before we returned to the lakeside, and I made my way slowly back to Brookhill, with aching limbs.

The charcoal burners, whom I saw daily, were short in stature but very sturdy. They collected sticks which they put in a long sack. A rope goes around the bottom of the sack and up over the head so that the weight is supported by the neck muscles. In those days there was no iodine in their diet and all of them had a goitre, some as large as a football. They spend all their lives in the mountains and are a quiet and kindly people. I once took a party of mountaineers, who were on their way to Nandi Devi, as far as Ashrams, about thirty six miles north of Naini, before I had to turn back. Although I started back with a full bottle of water it soon went. I had learnt a long time ago never to drink water from a stream however clear and clean it appeared to be; there was always the possibility it had been contaminated further upstream. I had come without a receptacle to boil water and had no matches. My mouth became very dry and my tongue started to swell. A charcoal burner noticed I was in trouble and said,

"Why don't you eat wild cucumber? You won't need water, for it will quench your thirst."

"I don't know what wild cucumber looks like," I replied.

"It's everywhere, come with me," he said.

A few paces further on we came across what looked like a marrow; it was over a foot long and about six inches thick. Puting down his load of sticks, he cut it from the stem and took slices from the cucumber, giving them to me to eat. I have always found cucumber rather bland but on this occasion it was like nectar from heaven and I have been indebted to the little old man ever since.

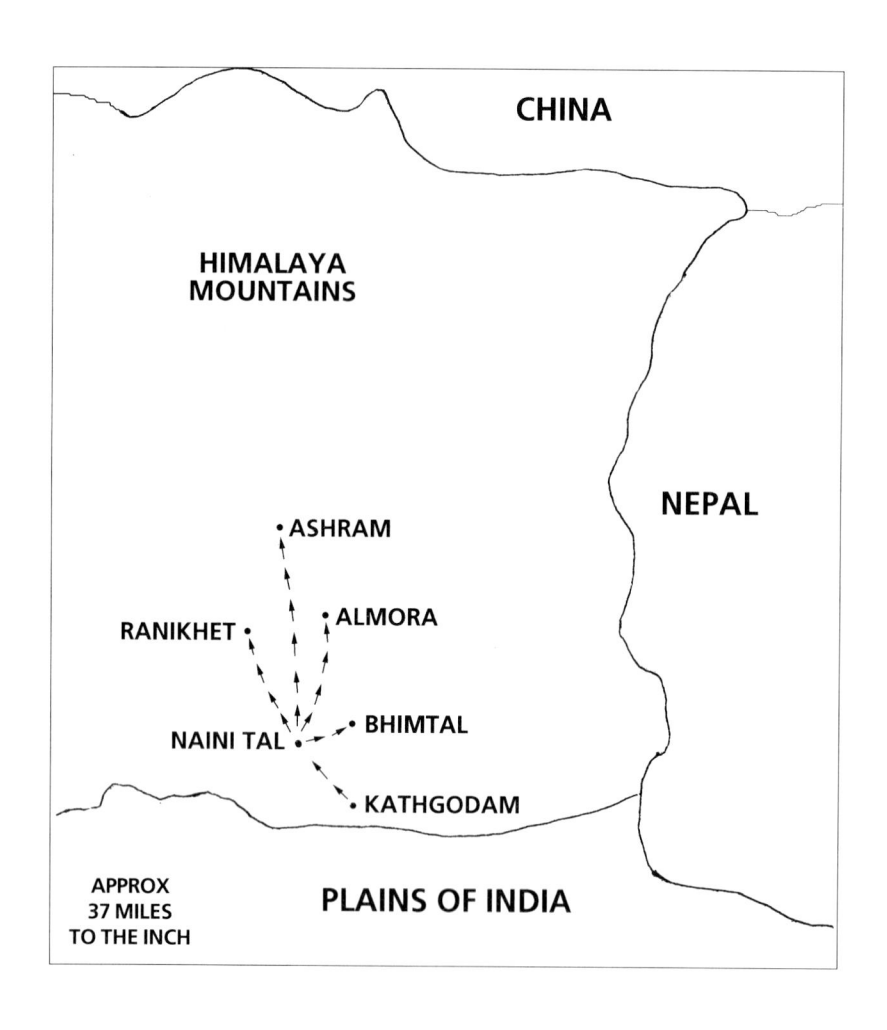

Chapter 16

Holidays in Naini Tal

I first met the Dunns in the summer of 1942 when they arrived at Brookhill Guest House where I stayed during the school holidays. At the time, Nick was nine and Philippa (Pip) was five. Pip was very pretty with fair skin and lovely long blonde hair which was often plaited in a pigtail. Because of our age difference, Nick and I saw little of each other during term time but were virtually inseparable during the holidays.

Brookhill was situated at the base of Mount Cheena, some distance from the lakeside. Most of the rooms were small except for the lounge and dining room. There were large grounds that were well kept. In the summer it was full, mainly with elderly people who came to the hills to avoid the intense heat of the plains. In winter it was empty except for a few old ladies but, also Betty Dunn and her two children. Jimmy Pointon also stayed there for a time and was joined by her husband, Peter, for two weeks leave. Before the war in the Far East, Peter worked for the Bombay Burma Trading Corporation in Bangkok, but was now on active service within Force 136, fighting the Japanese. Arthur Dunn, Betty's husband, who before the war had been employed on the Burma Railways, was also fighting on the Burma front.

Both Jimmy and Betty were very kind to me, Jimmy because of her connection with my parents, whom she knew, while Betty treated me as though I was her own son. So it was not surprising that Nick and I got on well together. In fact Nick and I shared the same bedroom while we were staying at Brookhill.

There were three school holidays during the year. The longest in the winter months from mid December to mid March when the weather could be bitterly cold and snow would pile up on the surrounding mountains. There was a two week holiday mid June and a further two weeks mid September.

Brookhill Guest House, Naini Tal

Nick, Pip and me at Brookhill 1943

After school had closed in December 1942 I went to Ranikhet about eighteen miles from Naini. Topsy Bailley, the proprietor of the guest house, said it would be nice to have mistletoe for Christmas and the best place to get it from was Ranikhet, where it grew in great profusion as a parasite in many of the trees. As I had no idea of how to get to Ranikhet, and unaware that there was a road, which was never mentioned, the proprietor instead introduced me to a small, heavily lined, but wiry old man called Rai. "Every Christmas, Rai goes to Ranikhet to collect mistletoe with a party of friends," said the proprietor, "He will show you the way."

Early one morning our little party of five Indians and myself set off. It was gently snowing but we were well wrapped up against the weather. The sun soon warmed the air and the snow did not settle. Rai, the leader of our group, spoke English. He said he was seventy years old, which I found very difficult to believe, in view of his amazingly agility. He also claimed to have been the Head Huntsman to the late Lord Irwin, Viceroy of India, until he grew too old for the job, but even then he was still a crack shot with a gun. The only thing that I carried was an army water bottle, my scout staff and plenty of warm clothing as I was warned that it might get very cold. The rest carried at their waist a bag of rice, curry, tea, some very primitive cooking utensils and a skinning knife and all were armed with shotguns.

Without hurrying we travelled at a steady pace. By midday our leader thought it was about time we ate and so we started to move slowly and stealthily through the undergrowth; nothing was said so as not to attract attention. A few minutes later, we lay low while Rai crept forward on all fours. Suddenly he raised his gun, a shot rang out and we all got up. As I had not seen anything move I presumed he had missed his prey. How wrong I was. We approached by a circular route and there lying dead was a kakkar, a small deer, shot in the head. One of the Indians started to skin the animal while others gathered up brushwood for a fire. Water was gathered from a nearby stream and boiled over the fire. The kakkar was jointed and pieces put in the pot. In another container rice was boiled and curry added. When our cook judged the meat to be ready it was added to the curried rice and we all ate with our fingers. I found it surprisingly tasty, if somewhat tough.

Our meal over, we set off again along the forest track. We either went up, or down, but seldom ever on the level. From time to time I caught a glimpse of the huge mountain range that is the Himalayas. Occasionally we jumped over a little stream that rushed down the hillside, disappearing in the undergrowth and then re-appearing further down where a small landslide had swept away the vegetation. The sun was now getting low and our leader said we would look for a suitable place to stop for the night. Presently we came across a huge oak, its branches forming a canopy. It was an ideal spot with an outstanding view. By now the sun was fast setting behind the mountains sixty to seventy miles north. As the last of the evening descended, the sun's rays changed from yellow to orange. The colours reflected off the snow-covered peaks which looked like huge jagged teeth enveloped in a ball of fire. In the distance came the muffled rumble of an avalanche. Above, the clouds were orange, red and grey as the snow once more started to fall.

The left over midday meal was re-heated and, when we had eaten, each of us found a comfortable spot to lie down for the night. A root of the oak served me well as a pillow. We settled down to sleep in the open with one man remaining on guard. During the night the Indians took turns guarding our little group. I was not asked to share this duty, which was just as well. I awoke early in the morning to witness a wonderful sunrise. The peach coloured clouds slowly dissolving, warmed by the sun as it rose higher in the sky. A light frost had formed in the glade overnight and was beginning to thaw. The tops of young plants that had come to life in the Spring were bowed over by the cold, but were now starting to raise their heads to the sky at the dawn of a new day. Shafts of sunlight penetrated the glade and soon a patchwork of shadows covered the ground. A rustle in the undergrowth heralded the awakening of small unseen animals.With all this beauty what more could anyone ask for.

After a quick cup of tea we were again on our way, walking steadily up and down the forest paths. Occasionally other paths crossed our way, but it became quite obvious to me that my friends had done this trip many times and knew every inch of the surrounding countryside. We reached Ranikhet at around three in the afternoon and immediately looked for trees with mistletoe. We did not have to look far as it grew everywhere. Three of the Indians climbed into the trees and threw down the mistletoe which the rest of us collected into six bundles which we placed in old, rather dirty, cotton squares which we had brought for this purpose. The diagonally opposite corners of each square we tied together for ease of carrying.

My Indian friends were well known in Ranikhet and one of them introduced me to an elderly Englishman who lived in a rather dilapidated cottage. He was stocky, with grey hair and a weather beaten face. Jock, for that was his name, had fallen in love with Ranikhet from the very first time he saw it some twenty years earlier and had decided to stay. He kindly gave me a meal and allowed me to sleep the night on his sofa.

I was up early next morning to join my colleagues. Each of us had a bundle of mistletoe to carry and I carried mine over my shoulder. The return journey to Naini Tal was uneventful but I wondered what the others would do with their mistletoe as I felt sure they would not use it for Christmas festivities. Rai said they would be taking it to the bus station and would be well paid for their trouble. As far as he knew it would be sent by bus to Kathgodam and then on to the cities where it was much in demand at this time of the year.

At Brookhill Guest House, on Christmas Day, mistletoe hung from every light in all the ground floor rooms. Being very shy by nature I kept well away as I did not want to be embarrassed.

Almora

During the summer holiday of 1943 I visited Almora. There was no particular reason for going except that the five Indians who had taken me with them to Ranikhet thought I might enjoy the walk. As we had done on the previous occasion, we left Naini early in the morning. The sun was rising above the mountain peaks and the air was wonderfully cool; the monsoon was not expected for at least another two weeks.

Almora lies northeast of Naini and although we left by the same route as when going to Ranikhet we soon turned off on another forest track. Our pattern of progress was similar to when we visited Ranikhet. The path inevitably went either up or down; the vegetation was a mixture of deciduous and pine trees. To my surprise some of the magnolia and rhododendrons, standing sixty feet high, were still resplendent in their huge magnificent blooms. Despite the undulations of the land we were gradually going downhill, as Almora is roughly one thousand feet lower than Naini and is reputed to be below the mosquito line and subject to poisonous snakes, although I never saw either during my brief visit. As we walked we came across a large tree that had much of its bark torn off. My immediate reaction was that there must be a tiger in the area and that it had been here recently as the marks were new. However, on looking at the pug marks on the ground, I concluded it was probably a mountain bear. After he had made a careful examination of the marks and the surrounding area, Rai said, "A bear is nearby, those pug marks were recently made, less than an hour ago and like us, it's travelling north. We must make a detour to avoid surprising it as bears can be fearsome." Travelling in silence, we left the track and continued through the undergrowth, which slowed our progress. Half an hour later we returned to the track and increased our speed to make up for lost time. There was no sign of the bear. Rai shot another kakkar; we dined, and proceeded on our way until evening, when Rai selected another tree beneath which we were to sleep; Salim was to take the first shift of guard duty.

It must have been around midnight when a shot rang out and I sat up with a start. Rai came over to Cook, who was on guard duty at the time and said, "What have you seen?" By this time I was beginning to understand a bit of the local dialect and what I did not comprehend I could infer. Our cook pointed, and lying on the ground on the fringes of the clearing was a large, dark object. We all got up and cautiously approached the object. However, caution as it happened was not necessary for lying dead on the ground was a Himalayan black bear with long, pointed claws. I turned to Rai and said,

"Could this be the same bear we avoided yesterday?"

"Probably," he replied. "They are fearful of man and very dangerous as they usually go for the face, and with those claws they can tear you apart in no time."

"Is that why you always choose to sleep below a tree where there is open ground all round as it allows our guard time to shoot any approaching aggressor?"

"Yes," he replied.

There was no further excitement that night and the next day we continued as before and arrived in Almora in the afternoon.

Unlike Naini or Ranikhet, Almora has a long history and has been inhabited for hundreds of years. On the highest point above Almora is a fort built during the time of the Chand dynasty and named Fort Nanda Devi. From here I could look down on the town and have a panoramic view of the Himalayas and in particular Nanda Devi itself, the world's fifth highest mountain, from which the fort took its name. This whole area is where the Gurkhas come from. There is an old Ghurka battle song commemorating their defeat of the Sikhs at Naini Tal, that goes as follows, written phonetically to represent Ghurkhali:

> *Naini Ta-a-la ee Naini Tala*) Naini Tal, repeated four times
> *Naini Ta-a-la ee Naini Tala*)
> *Gum-ay ai-o ray-ilo*) They go round and round and
> *Gum-ay ai-o ray-ilo*) about, repeated twice
> *Aukha ma launay kalo gudgal*) In your eyes there is a black look
> *Bul-bul laya matiha*) I catch you by the beard
> *Naini Tal.*

That night we all slept out in the open in a small garden of a retired Gurkha army friend of Rai's. Usually I had no difficulty in sleeping on the ground, but that night was an exception. I got up while it was still dark and made my way to the fort from where I could see the mountains. Suddenly, a shooting star streaked through the night its light reflecting off the distant snow covered peaks like a firework display, then suddenly it seemed to stop directly over Nanda Devi, and in a brilliant flash that illuminated the surrounding peaks, burnt itself out. I stood transfixed on the fortifications above Almora marvelling at my luck at seeing such a phenomenon.

I remained gazing at the mountains as the sun slowly rose, the darkened Himalayan peaks silhouetted against the early morning light. Above, the clouds were salmon pink while the fertile valley below was beginning to wake as the damp ground first reflected, then dissolved in the sun's rays. I returned to my friends who were already up and making tea. After a hasty breakfast we started on the return journey to Naini which was uneventful, taking two days and a night.

Shortly after my return from Almora, Topsy Bailly said,

"Would you mind very much sleeping in a tent for a couple of weeks as the guest house is full up with visitors who have been unable to find alternative accomodation?"

"No," I replied, "I used to go camping very often in Sumatra and am quite used to sleeping in a tent."

The ground on which the tent was pitched sloped down toward the lake. It had been erected so that the canvas covering did not reach the earth at any point, but it was a large tent supported by two thick poles and held in place with guy ropes. My camp bed had long legs so that all bedding was well clear of the ground. A small but adequate chest of drawers for my meagre belongings rested well above ground level and was secured to one of the tent poles. The reason for all this preparation became obvious a few days later when the monsoon broke. Rain water rushed down the hillside straight through the tent and out the other side. Lying in bed at night watching the water as it passed below me was great fun and in many ways I regretted having to return indoors once the visitors had left.

From time to time Naini suffered a slight tremor which usually caused minor landslides. On one occasion the lake turned a muddy yellow colour and dead fish came floating to the surface. Sometimes, I would go rowing on the lake and used to think that I was a proficient oarsman, that is until John said to me as I was getting out of my boat one day,

"Would you like me to show you how to row without making heavy weather of it?" I felt deflated, but said "Yes please."

He got into the boat and showed me how to feather the oars which made rowing much easier. John claimed that he had been a rowing blue at Oxford University in his younger days.

In the winter of 1942 after the school had closed for holidays, I went down with mumps a few days after Christmas. Nick and I were immediately isolated and told to remain in our room and on no account to go into any other part of the building except to the adjoining bathroom. Betty would bring in our meals on a tray. As we were always hungry we supplemented our meals by toasting bread in front of the electric fire in the room. At first my neck felt quite sore and it was painful to turn my head and to swallow, but despite the swelling on both sides of the neck, I quickly threw it off.

Unfortunately, on the last day of my isolation, Nick went down with mumps, so much of the holiday was spent on our own.

Until this happened and apart from my trip to Ranikhet, Nick and I spent most of our time together except for some evenings when I made up a foursome at Mah Jong with three elderly ladies. At first I was confused by the way they played and said,

"Why do you turn over the bricks once discarded? They should remain face downwards."

" We have always played this way and know of no other," replied one of the ladies.

They liked to play for money but, as I pleaded bankruptcy, they very kindly offered to pay for my losses and said that I could keep my winnings. I soon discovered that their idea of the game was simple compared with the way I had been taught in Siam, which was very much to my advantage. I don't think they ever really understood why I won so often. Anyway, in appreciation they gave me a pack of 'Happy Families' playing cards for Christmas. It was a kind jesture but it reminded me of the last Christmas I spent in Sumatra and when alone I could not help recall the happy times I had with my parents and brother before the Japanese entered the war in the Far East, and it made me feel very sad.

I think that Betty Dunn realised what I was going through and on Boxing Day she took me to her room and said,

"Don't be too downhearted. When the war is over we would very much like you to join our family and to treat Arthur and me as your own parents, and Nick and Pip as your brother and sister."

I could no longer contain myself and burst out crying. I felt ashamed at having let go but very quickly got my feelings under control.

"Thank you so much," I said, and put my arms around her and gave her a hug.

"You must not tell this to anyone," she said "at least not for the time being. I have already mentioned it to Arthur and he thinks it an excellent idea but we shall have to wait until this dreadful war is over before we can make any decisions for the future. We may return to Burma; on the other hand, we could go back to England."

This was a load off my mind; at least I would be with a family that I loved. I could not remember what family I had in England apart from grandparents, uncles and aunts whom I seldom saw.

Chapter 17

A letter from the dead.

Until now the only letters I ever received, and they were few, were from Fay Williams in Ooty and from Tom Thomson, a member of the Friends Ambulance Unit who I had met in Calcutta; he was driving ambulances on the Burma Road and it was kind of him to write to me as he must have been busy looking after the injured and dying that he and his colleagues were trying to help.

Early in January 1943 when, much to my surprise, I received an airmail letter from Lourenço Marques in Portugese East Africa. It had been addressed to me in Bombay, opened by the censor and re-directed to the Hallett War School. With total incomprehension I opened it to see who had sent it and went wild with excitement. With disbelief I read the letter and another enclosed. It was from my mother and Jon; they were alive and so was my Father, though he remained behind in Bangkok. I was not, after all, an orphan.

Many years later my mother told me that, on arriving in Lourenço Marques she telephoned the Bombay Burma Trading Corporation head office in Bombay for news of my whereabouts. She was told that I was in India and so wrote to me via the company office in Bombay.

Although my mother had hoped that I could join her in Lourenco Marques, it was impossible. There was no way in which I could reach Bombay let alone Portugese East Africa before mother and Jon set sail for England. In October 1942 when Mother and Jon returned to the United Kingdom, they sent me a Christmas present, which eventually arrived on Christmas Eve 1943, the following year. Considering the rationing in England at the time I was surprised that it contained chocolates and biscuits all of which had gone mouldy. The biggest surprise was a yellow yo-yo made of wood. As yo-yos were the the current craze at school mine had arrived at just the right time and I was delighted.

Mother's letter from Lourenço Marques

Aug. 25th   On board S.S. Tatuta Maru

Darling Patrick,
                    I am wondering what arrangements are being made for you to join us. I do hope it will be possible. Jon & I are longing to have you with us again. Since leaving Bangkok I have sent two telegrams asking for you to be sent to Africa to join us at Lourenço Marques & return to England with us on this first evacuation. But unless you come by air it will be impossible for you to arrive in time. But in that case perhaps you can join the 2nd evacuation which they expect to be about November, if the B.B.T.C.L. were to say you can join that Jon & I will wait for you in Africa. It's very difficult to arrange, but it will be lovely if it can be fixed. Well darling, how are you? I'm longing for news & hope to get it at Lourenço Marques where we arrive on Aug 27th. Jon & I are well & so is Daddy. We are hoping Daddy will be evacuated

2.
on the next ship which starts from Tokyo in October, but it is not certain.
We did not have too bad a time in our internment camp, we were not ill treated in any way, but of course it was not very pleasant, we were behind barbed wire in a school building on the river front, & we had a tiny room or cubicle for the 3 of us & it was very boring & the food was not good. It was too bad Daddy could not come too, but this ship is chiefly for diplomats & only 35 ordinary people, mostly women & children, were taken from our camp.
On this boat we are travelling steerage — but we're lucky to be on it at all!
I am so glad you got out of Sumatra in good time & wonder how you like school in India. There is such a lot I want to know. I hope you've written me a long long letter! It will be lovely if you can manage to get to Africa in time for the 2nd ship, which I believe leaves Lourenco Marques about Sept 7th. However, even if you can't, you might come later & perhaps we shall all be together for Xmas.

3) Jon is well, he had measles while we were interned, but afterwards enjoyed having lots of other children to play with in the camp.
I was in hospital for a while with sciatica in my leg, but it is better now. If we go straight on to England I suppose we will live with, or near, Grandfather, but everything is so uncertain it is impossible to make plans. A great deal depends on Jon, & when you are likely to come.

You must have had lots of adventures & I am looking forward to hearing all your news.

We were shut up in our houses from Dec. 8 — to Dec. 23rd when we were interned & from then on nothing very exciting happened. We had several air raids, that is all. We heard we were to be exchanged only a few weeks before leaving. We left Bangkok on Aug 4th travelling by coastal steamer to Saigon (5 days) where we went on board this ship which is large 17,000 tons & very fast. Jon & I both were ill at first, but now we are quite well. We arrive in 2 days time, but will probably have to stay on board till the 30th before we are exchanged (for Japanese coming from England) It has been quite a pleasant trip, not really rough, & quite cold.

4/ I do not really want to stay in Africa, but if you can come later I will do so, but I do not know where I will be allowed to stay, probably not in Lourenco Marques which is Portuguese, we would have to go to South Africa I expect. If I get no message from you (or the B.B.T.C.L) in L.M. about joining me I will go on to England + try + arrange that you join Daddy when he is evacuated.

I wonder you you are, if you like India, is Jay at the same school, how is the asthma? Did you go to Bombay with Mr Williams. Mrs Williams is still in Bangkok. Only women with children + a few men were allowed to travel on this boat with the diplomats. We talk + think of you a lot + hope to see you very soon. Happy times darling. A whole heap of love from Daddy + Mummy + Jon. xxx.

For the next few days I was overjoyed, but as I got used to my new situation I began to feel that something was wrong, something kept nagging at me inside I could not understand what it was. I somehow felt that I should be even happier, even more elated, than I was. Gradually it dawned on me. I think that, in my subconscious, I had by now accepted the shock that I was an orphan and that my parents and brother were dead. I could no longer be hurt by my loss. Somehow I was part of another family and my old family was intruding. This acceptance had now been overturned. Would I really feel the same way toward them as I had once felt? They were alive, but would my old feelings return? When they came to die a second time how would I react, would I be as upset and weep to myself as I did on the first occasion? Doubts entered my mind. In September 1944 while in Sidmouth, mother received a phone call from Uncle Larry: father was dead. To me it did not come as a shock and I never shed a tear, the hurt had died in February 1942.

Return to Bombay

For the next 15 months life continued as usual. Betty was delighted that my parents were alive, and hoped that when the war was over our two families would meet again in England.

During the summer holiday of 1943, Arthur Dunn came to Naini on leave from the Burma front. The weather was pleasant and we had a picnic breakfast on the slopes of Mount Cheena where we could look down on the lake and admire the beauty of the surrounding hills in the early morning sunshine. The countryside was glorious, the huge deodar cedar trees, some standing well over 200 feet high, with pale green flowers and green fir cones, were a wonderful sight. We would collect cones that were lying on the ground and take them back to the guest house to be burnt in the winter, when they gave off a lovely scent of pine. Nick and I had seen little of the mountains opposite the Hallett War School, across the lake, so for the brief period that Arthur Dunn was with us, we explored Ayarpetta and visited Dorothy's Seat at Tiffin Top.

On one occasion a low-flying aircraft caused a number of minor landslides which could have been dangerous. Aeroplanes were not supposed to fly low over the hills and I was told that this particular plane crashed before it returned to base. The details were hushed up but we were informed that the pilot and crew were killed.

Picnic breakfast on Mount Cheena with the Dunns

I returned to school at the beginning of the Spring term in 1944, but stayed barely one month. Mr. Gibbons had managed to secure a passage for me back to England on a troopship. So I returned to Bombay in early March and fortunately for me the train didn't stop at the dreaded Muttra. I had expected to sail almost immediately, but had to curb my impatience. To while away the time, I went to Breach Candy and spent much of the day swimming, or fooling around with the many soldiers who were waiting for news of their next posting. The nights were cool and rather pleasant; I slept out on the upstairs verandah of the house with the parakeets which lived in the surrounding trees. When dawn broke these birds with their multi-coloured plumage would start calling to one another and I would watch them flying from tree to tree, which gave me great pleasure.

On the 14th April I was still in Bombay and as usual enjoying myself swimming, when at ten minutes past four in the afternoon there was a deafening explosion followed by a further explosion five minutes later which shook the ground; windows shattered in a few of the buildings near to the pool. An army officer appeared and shouted: "All forces personnel to report immediately to their barracks." I quickly dressed and returned to Armardale where Mr. and Mrs. Gibbons lived on Malabar Hill. Mrs. Gibbons was waiting for me and said, " An ammunition ship has blown up in the harbour and we may be asked to assist in some way, so please don't leave the house without telling me." As there was no request for help during the late afternoon and evening, I decided after supper to go to my room and read. The room by now was dark except for a bright light shining in through the windows. I went on to the verandah and to my astonishment I realised that the light was coming from the west, the other side of Malabar hill, which is where the docks are situated. Even though I could not see the flames, ash and other debris were visible in the sky. I settled down to read on the verandah; there was no need for a light for I could see perfectly well by the light of the fires.

A few minutes later Mrs. Gibbons came running upstairs and gasped, "Quickly, I've told my chauffeur to take you to the docks to help on a mobile canteen giving refreshments to the firefighters-you'll be told what to do when you arrive: Oh! do be quick." Hastily I put on my shoes, jumped into the waiting car, and in a short space of time was at the docks.

It was a scene of devastation and chaos. There were moored ships ablaze in the water and flames coming through the roofs of the godowns on the dockside. An additional hazard was the possibility of collapsing walls as the firemen tried their best to prevent this from happening. A naval ship had been lifted twenty feet on to the quayside. Sailors from the Royal Navy, Royal Indian Navy, airmen from the Royal Air Force and soldiers from the Army were running in every direction; trucks were being filled from godowns not yet on fire and driven away at high speed. Smoke and flames billowed from the hulks of burning ships and many of the godowns behind the dockside were also ablaze. Firemen lining the quayside were directing their hoses into the burning ships while others were doing their best to extinguish the fires raging in all the buildings along the road. Showers of sparks, like a firework display shot skyward and were blown into other parts of town where a large area of the city was burnt out.

Within minutes of my arrival, I was on a mobile canteen as we swept into this scene of havoc. There were three of us working together: a driver, another helper organising tea and sandwiches, and myself who had the job of taking the refreshments to the firefighters. The firefighters had been at the scene ever since the first explosion; perspiration poured off their faces and they all looked worn-out. The first man I approached was at the end of a plank, one end of which was on the quayside and the other on the burning ship, with his hose directed into the bowels of the vessel. The heat was intense. He was from the Royal Navy. I tapped him on the shoulder and he looked round.

"What the bloody hell are you doing here, do you want to be blown up? Get off immediately." I stood my ground.

"I'll get off when you have had this food and drink and not before," I said. He smiled when he saw what I was carrying.

"That's marvellous, I'm dying of thirst, give me the tea first, I hope it's not too hot. Put the sandwiches on the plank, thanks sonny, and now get the hell out of here before you end up as one of the dead or wounded."

I was glad to get away, it was so hot. Even some six hours after the inital explosions an occasional shell could be heard blowing up in the holds of many of the ships tied up along the quay. I soon got into a kind of rhythm dashing from the mobile canteen to a firefighter and back again. Not surprisingly they all asked for a drink first. When we had run out of supplies we returned to base, got into another vehicle which was ready waiting full of refreshments, and dashed back to the dockside. The organisation was terrific. As a team we continued like this for thirty six hours non-stop, by which time I was dead on my feet, covered in grime with sweat pouring down my face. I never discovered the name of the first man I served, but each time I gave him further sustenance we had a good laugh together. I began to understand what it must have been like for those poor people back in Britain during the blitz, who kept up their morale in spite of everything that the German Luftwaffe could throw at them.

The cause of the carnage in Bombay was a British ammunition ship, the Fort Stikine, which caught fire and blew up. Fires spread to Prince's Dock and raged all night. A total of 18 merchant vessels and three Indian naval vessels were destroyed. Two docks were burnt out as well as a large part of the city. Three hundred and thirty six people were reported killed and one thousand and forty injured. Half the grain stocks held in Bombay were estimated to have been lost. Most of the grain was housed in godowns on the dockside as well as a road a short distance from where the ships had been moored. As I came off duty I met an Indian limping, his arm in a sling, and we chatted for a few minutes. He said that he was riding a motorcycle along the front when the first explosion occurred and was blown right over the buildings, landing on sacks of grain the other side, which broke his fall. He was lucky to be alive and to suffer only a broken arm.

    I was given a lift back to Malabar Hill, walked up the drive to Armadale and knocked on the door. There was a long pause before the door opened. There stood Mrs. Gibbons, she hesitated then realised who I was and let me in. "Take your shoes off, go upstairs and have a bath, I'll arrange for clean clothes to be put on your bed." That night nothing could have woken me up.

R.M.S. Otranto

Chapter 18

ss Otranto

Shortly after the fires in the Bombay docks the dhobi wallah (washerman) employed by Mrs. Gibbons came up to me while I was walking in the garden and said,
"Please, Sahib, my wife and I would consider it a great honour if you could come to the wedding of our son in three weeks' time." I was taken aback because the dhobi wallah was so young, so I said,
"How old is your son?"
"Six, and his bride-to-be is four," he replied.
Although I had always got on very well with all the servants employed by the Gibbons this request came as a great shock. I was momentarily lost for words. I hesitated, wondering what to reply, and then said,
"It is a most kind invitation and the honour is mine, but I fear that I may shortly be on my way back to England. Could I let you know when I have some news?"

He bowed and went on his way. When I next met Mrs. Gibbons I told her of the invitation which she dismissed with a flourish of her hand. " The servants are always asking us to attend various events, they feel obliged to, but we never go." I didn't argue the point with her but inwardly I felt she should at least sometimes make the effort for the sake of her staff.

Three days later Mr. Gibbons asked me to come into his study.
"You will be sailing on the ss Otranto the day after tomorrow – we shall be sorry to see you go, but I am sure you will be very happy to see your mother and brother and to go to school in England."
"Thank you," I said. "Have you got any news of my father?"

"No, regrettably, as you are already aware, his repatriation from Bangkok along with other internees, never materialised, and to the best of our knowledge they are still in the same camp near one of the bridges over the Menan River. Your mother will be kept advised by our London office if there is a change in the situation."

Two days later I said goodbye to Mr. and Mrs. Gibbons, thanked them for all they had done for me, and was taken by their chauffeur to the docks. On our way I asked the chauffeur to say goodbye on my behalf to all the other servants and to tell them that it had been a privilege to know them and especially to thank the dhobi wallah for his kind invitation to the marriage of his son.

The dockside was crowded with troops all waiting for orders to board ship. When the signal was given, soldiers in full battle kit started up the gangway. It was a slow process as each had to be ticked off on a rota before stepping aboard. The army personnel were followed by the men from the R.A.F. While this was going on I took a gentle stroll around the place making a mental farewell to Bombay. Eventually, it was the turn of the civilians, of whom there were relatively few.

I clutched the small blue KLM suitcase that had now accompanied me for many years and proceeded up the gangway. I had no other belongings apart from what I stood up in. Such things as trunks were not permitted; there were other items of much greater importance to fill the ship's hold. Signs had been posted up to guide passengers to their sleeping quarters, dining room, bar, and other parts of the ship. As there were so many people milling about I gave up the struggle and went to relax in what had once been a lounge. It was now very austere; any sign of luxury had gone. I sat here for an hour until a voice over the ship's tannoy system brought me to my feet. "Would master P.M.R. Gibson report immediately to the Pursar's office on B Deck." I found the office and knocked on the door. A voice said, "Come in." I entered a small room. On the opposite side from the door, a man in naval uniform sat behind a large desk, with another man standing in front of him, talking. The man standing with his back to me was in a blue uniform with a lot of scrambled egg on his epaulettes and hat, which was under his arm. I paused, not wishing to interrupt. When they had finished, the officer turned around. I was astounded. It was my uncle Larry. He grinned, "I just thought it might be you," he said. "There can't be many P.M.R. Gibsons in this world. You will be joining me in my cabin so you had better behave yourself or you'll have to sleep in a hammock like the rest of the troops."

Larry had changed little since I saw him last as a Squadron Leader at Duxford. He had become a little puffy in the face, no doubt due to an excess of alcohol, for he had always enjoyed his gin and tonic. After the Captain of the ship, my uncle was apparently the most senior officer on board. By now he was Group Captain and he would be in charge of all the anti-aircraft guns on the port side of the ship, as we expected enemy action. As the Otranto was the most heavily-armed merchant ship in the convoy she would be positioned in the centre. I never discovered how many ships were actually in the convoy, but rumours varied from sixty to one hundred and twenty nine. On the Otranto, we would be carrying two thousand British troops and four thousand Italian prisoners of war; the latter were placed at the stern of the ship. Amongst the Italians were the complete orchestra from La Scala, Milan with all their instruments, except for a grand piano. Where they were caught and what they had been doing in India, I have no idea. Among the British troops was the Ralph Reader Gang Show.

It was late in April that the convoy set sail under cover of darkness. I assumed we would be going via South Africa, but my Uncle would not tell me anything about the route. By the morning I was suffering from asthma again so reported to the ship's doctor. He had nothing he could give me except for ephedrine tablets which made me feel dreadful. They did not help in the slightest. Larry said "Why don't you throw them overboard? They are obviously useless." So I did.

On board there were none of the facilities you would expect to find on a peace time luxury liner no quoits, badminton, swimming pool; no first or second class areas; no cabins, except for the Captain and my Uncle, just rows and rows of hammocks on each deck. What had at one time been lounges and dining rooms were now austere, utilitarian, and devoid of any semblance of comfort. None of this mattered as the troops were happy to be returning to Blighty and laughed and joked together; no doubt they had had to put up with far greater hardship since the commencement of the war.

We were now somewhere in the Indian Ocean, the weather wonderful and the sun very hot. In front of us in convoy was the

Strathnaver, to stern the Strathaird, on our port side the Queen of Bermuda and on the starboard side the Empress of Australia. They were all beautiful liners. Beyond, as far as the eye could see, were other ships large and small. The course set by the convoy leader constantly varied; we zig zagged, slowed down or went full steam ahead while destroyers sailed in and out of the merchant ships. Our speed was dependant on the slowest vessel in the convoy.

Both sides of the Otranto were fitted with Oerlikon anti-aircraft guns while on the stern stood a six-inch gun. Among the British troops was a company from the Royal Artillery. They were detailed to man the guns, two for each Oerlikon, and three for the six-inch gun on the stern. As they had no previous experience of firing from a moving and rolling ship, training started on the very first day. An aeroplane trailing a drogue appeared as if from nowhere and the anti-aircraft guns started blazing away. The drogue was soon in shreds. Another was slowly let out from the rear of the plane. When the order was given to fire a cockney voice shouted, "Let's go for the tow rope, the drogue is too easy." The rope was severed almost immediately, with lots of cheering as it fell to the sea. Next it was the turn of the three operating the six-inch gun. A smoke float was lowered over the side of the ship and the vessels to our stern moved out of the way. The first shot was fired when the float was six miles away, and landed in the water, causing the float to rock backwards and forwards. The second landed on the other side of the float. By now the float had disappeared over the horizon but the smoke could be plainly seen. The chief gunner rubbed his hands together, spat in them and shouted, "This time we'll get the bastard." By now everyone was watching. The elevation of the gun was raised a fraction: "Fire" yelled the chief gunner. The gun exploded into action and a second later the float blew up in a dense cloud of smoke. A destroyer signalled a direct hit and everyone cheered.

Among the civilians on board was a boy of eight, together with his parents who were taking him to England to further his education. They had come from Australia. Unfortunately the boy had managed to pick up an infection which there was no means of treating on board ship and he died three days after leaving Bombay. There followed a very moving service led by the ship's padre and attended by many of the troops. As the bugler played 'The Last Post' the child's body slipped from beneath the Union Jack and was committed to the deep. It had been a very moving scene and even some of the hardened soldiers had tears in their eyes.

On board there was little I could do except to stroll around the decks and watch the sea. I got out my yo-yo which was bright yellow, one of the items from my mother's Christmas parcel that had arrived over a year late. It had a twelve-foot length of string on it so I played with it over the side of the ship. I was quite expert at the yo-yo, throwing it out in front of me, letting it return over, then under, my hand as it sped out to the full length of the string before returning once again. I had been playing in this way for a few minutes when a soldier came up to me and said,

"How would you like to do that on the stage, sonny?" I have always been shy and said, "I wouldn't."

"You'd give a lot of people a great deal of pleasure," said the soldier.

"I'd be much too frightened to do it in front of an audience," I replied, and never took part in the entertainment. The soldier turned out to be Ralph Reader. He led a variety show which was very popular with the troops during the war.

When night fell all the ships were blacked out; the only sound was that of the ship's engine and the spray from the ship's bow as it cut through the water. From time to time, signalmen's lights could be seen flashing instructions from one vessel to the next.

On the second night out from Bombay entertainment was provided by Ralph Reader's Gang Show. It was a variety performance and extremely popular. The room was packed and those not fortunate enough to get a seat stood wherever they could find a space. The VIPs like the captain, first mate, my uncle and a few others, sat in the front row and were subjected to many wisecracks from the performers. The applause and cheering was deafening. I can remember only one verse of an act performed by two men that went:

A cock may crow the whole night through
And strut about all day,
But, he's beat when it comes to laying an egg
Why? because he ain't built that way.

There were, needless to say, many well known war time songs, like:

Run rabbit, run rabbit, run run run.
Pack up your troubles in your old kit bag.
She'll be wearing silk pyjamas when she comes.
We're going to hang up the washing on the Siegfried line.

And many more. The troops joined in with great gusto, but the greatest applause came when the Gang Show played, 'We're riding along on the crest of a wave'.The noise was so great that one of the escort ships told us to be quieter.

The Gang Show performed on alternate nights and the room was always packed. As the afternoon light was beginning to fade, the Italians from La Scala, not to be outdone, arranged chairs on the stern of the ship and sat down to play. Their first piece was the Blue Danube followed by a series of popular tunes interspersed with classical music. A metal barrier separated the orchestra from the British troops and armed guards strolled backwards and forwards along the barrier. The music wafting over the water as the sun set in a blaze of glory was magical. Who would have thought there was a war which still had to be won?

Home at last

As we crossed the Indian Ocean the convoy became more strung out, with the faster ships leading. After leaving Bombay we did not sight land until the fifth day. At first it appeared like a creamy white sheet reflecting the rays of the sun on the starboard side of the ship. We got closer and I recognised Aden in the distance, but there was no stopping to pick up supplies, or to repeat the coach ride which I had enjoyed on my way out East in 1938. By now I was very surprised, as we were presumably to sail through the Red Sea and Suez Canal, where we would be sitting ducks for enemy aircraft. We sailed up the Red Sea in daylight entering the Suez Canal as the sun set. I kept an eye out for the sweet water canal and the dredgers that keep it open to shipping. We passed through it by the grey light of night. In the morning when I awoke we were in the Mediterranean and it was a beautiful day. Our speed was reduced to allow the other ships to catch up; the naval destroyers kept going backwards and forwards at full steam like Welsh border collies rounding up cattle. The Italians on board instinctively knew they were near home and before we knew it, La Scala were back on deck with more wonderful music. Before long a German reconnaissance plane was sighted and the anti-aircraft guns opened up with a barrage that caused the plane to turn tail and run. After this brief encounter we expected a raid by enemy aircraft; emergency drill was tightened up and we were forever putting on and taking off our life-jackets. However, nothing happened. We sailed through the Straits of Gibralter when it was dark and out into the Atlantic. I didn't sight land again until we reached Liverpool. I assumed the convoy probably sailed to the West of Ireland, approaching Liverpool from the North, but no mention was made of our route. On reaching land we had to wait outside the harbour for three days, due to German U-boats, which were reputedly active in the area.

Eventually, we disembarked at Liverpool but had to wait on the dockside preparatory to going through Customs. Even during the war there was strict control of everyday items that one was allowed to bring in. As a senior officer my uncle would be one of the first allowed through. Along the dockside was a temporary movable metal barrier about six feet high with an opening in the middle where Customs officers stood to examine anything they thought might be suspicious. I then got quite a shock. Larry said, "You go through Customs first so that I can hand things over the barrier to you, as I have more than my limit on cigarettes, sugar, soap, and other contraband." As he spoke we were standing about ten feet from the Customs officers. I did what I was told and as I had nothing to declare I was waved straight through. Larry started to hand over the top of the barrier the whole contents of a medium-sized trunk. It mostly consisted of gin and cigarettes, both of which he was passionately fond. All this time the Custom officials watched without a murmur. In fact one officer offered to help. Having now depleted his stocks to the permitted amount, Larry went through Customs without challenge.

An R.A.F. corporal took the baggage to a jeep which was waiting to take us to Lime Street station. On arrival, the corporal placed Larry's belongings in the guards van and about half an hour later we were off. It was late afternoon on the 1st June, 1944. We spoke little on the train; Larry had already telephoned my Mother to meet us at Euston. I think I spent most of the journey either gazing out of the window or asleep. Larry tried writing a report, which I suspect was illegible due to the motion of the train.

ORIENT   LINE

BREAKFAST

OATMEAL PORRIDGE   WHEAT FLAKES

SCRAMBLED EGG ON FRIED BREAD

GRILLED BACON

SAUTÉ POTATOES

TEA   COFFEE   PRESERVE

LUNCHEON

POTAGE HOTCHPOT

OX TAIL SOUBISE

COLD MEATS

MASHED POTATOES
CARROTS

BOILED SULTANA ROLL

DINNER

CRÊME DE RIZ

FILLET OF COD, SALAMANDRE

ROAST RIBS OF BEEF

BROWNED AND BOILED POTATOES
CABBAGE

CARAMEL CREAMS

THURSDAY, JUNE 1ST, 1944

Children's Menu

□ □ □

BREAKFAST

STEWED PEACHES

OATMEAL PORRIDGE   WHEAT FLAKES

SCRAMBLED EGG

LUNCHEON

VEGETABLE SOUP

COTTAGE PIE

MASHED POTATOES WITH GRAVY

CARROTS

BREAD AND BUTTER CUSTARD

DINNER

CLEAR SOUP

POACHED FISH

MASHED POTATOES WITH GRAVY

CABBAGE

CARAMEL CREAMS

THURSDAY, JUNE 1ST, 1944

The last menu before the Otranto docked at Liverpool

It was getting dark when the train pulled in to Euston. Larry and I got out and made our way to the ticket barrier while a porter brought my small suitcase and all Larry's luggage. Mother and Jon were waiting by the barrier. I looked at them both with a strange kind of hesitation, I can't remember why. It seemed that I was asking myself a question: is this really my mother and brother or is it all in the imagination? Considering what I had gone through since I had last seen them, I found it difficult to believe my eyes. Mother broke the silence,

"You look awful," she said, "Just as though you had come from an internment camp. Didn't they feed you in India?"

I went up to my mother, kissed her and gave her a big hug, and shook hands with Jon.

"As a matter of fact," I said, " In the last three months I have put on nearly three stone in weight."

Larry departed and we took a taxi to Bayswater where mother and Jon were staying with my grandparents.

On arriving at Moscow Road, Margaret Hubbard, my grandmother and step-grandfather Raymond were delighted to see me. After the usual exchange of greetings and affection we sat down to a light supper. The meal over Raymond had to go on air raid precaution duty on the roof of the block of flats where they lived. I decided to look around their flat; very little had changed since I was last there in the Spring of 1938. The stone coloured walls looked a bit dirtier. The runner that lay on the corridor floor from the front door to the lounge and came from Russia was now badly worn and in places there were holes. Its original rich red colour had faded into an orange-brown dullness. The wainscot that ran either side of the corridor was badly chipped. Much to my surprise the pair of silver Georgian candlesticks were still on either end of the mantlepiece over the fire-place, though they had not been polished for years. The kitchen had not changed since I last saw it and it brought back memories of my uncle Humphrey drying dishes in the adjoining room, as the kitchen was too small to accomodate two people at the same time.

And so my first day back in England slowly drew to a close. By now I was exhausted both emotionally and physically. As I lay in bed reflecting on the past few years, I knew that this was the end of the road, I was home. As I fell asleep I heard the distant sound of air raid sirens, but for me it was oblivion.

Chapter 19

My parents' story (as related to me by my mother 50 years after the ending of World War 2.)

The Association of British Civilian Internees, Far East Region, asked me to represent my father – who had been put to death by the Japanese – in the commemorative parade of veterans on August 19th 1995, the 50th anniversary of the ending of the war in the Far East. It was only when I mentioned this request to my mother, Charlotte Gibson, that for the first time she could bring herself to talk to me about the events that took place when the Japanese entered Bangkok in December 1941. From internment in their own house on 8th December they were moved to the University of Moral and Political Science two weeks later. There were threats of rape, and shooting. They coped as best they could with help from Ayah Lamduan. Mother and Jon were eventually released nine months later. Then in August 1944 we learnt of the death of my father at the hands of the Japanese. Previously, if approached, she would never talk about what had happened, and would immediately change the subject. Since the 50th anniversary it has taken me more than 18 months of diplomatic questioning to get to the truth. The following represents what my parents and other internees went through.

After the Japanese occupied Indo China in 1941, without declaring war, the British Minister in Bangkok, Josiah Crosby, warned all British citizens to leave Siam. These warnings were repeated on more than one occasion but, as nothing happened, those who had left began to drift back to Bangkok. Consequently, the majority of British who resided in the Capital were caught and interned by the Japanese. A few did get away, but those who escaped were mainly resident in Chieng Mai. The two grandsons of Anna Leonowens (the real life Anna) heeded these warnings and left Siam before war broke out in the Far East.

In the autumn of 1941 my parents, and Jon, now eight, went for a holiday to New Zealand as it was not possible to visit England because of the war in Europe. They returned to Bangkok in October and my mother, together with other mothers, began making things for the Red Cross for a sale, which was due to be held on 10th December. It never took place and the Japanese were the only beneficiaries. At this time I was still at school in Sumatra.

On the 7th December my parents attended a ball at the British Club, a combination of the Annual Winter dance, a postponed St. Andrews Dance, and a fête, in aid of the Red Cross. Mother wore a blue taffeta gown and silver coloured high heeled shoes. Athole Brose, a mixture of whisky, honey and oatmeal, served from a barrel, went down very well. They were enjoying themselves when a Reuters correspondent, Mr. S.A. Ayer, a particular friend of my mother, rushed in, took my mother aside and told her that the Japanese had just bombed Pearl Harbour. He said, "You must leave immediately, and go by the Three Pagoda Route, otherwise it will be too late." My parents went straight home.

The Three Pagoda Route goes through the mountains to Burma, and only the physically fit are able to endure a forced march through the jungle, but the trek is out of the question for a child.

Mr Ayer, after his warning, left immediately with a friend, taking a train from Bangkok to Banpong where they joined a group of other people trying to get away. On his return to England, two years later, he told my mother that they then took a lorry to Kanchanaburi on the river Kwai Noi. From there they travelled by boat upstream for thirty-six hours, but on the way they learnt from local villagers that the Three Pagoda Route was full of Siamese police and troops. The group held a meeting and decided to leave the boat a few miles short of the Pass and to proceed through the jungle. The two fittest men went on ahead in the hope of finding assistance in Tavoy on the Burmese side of the border with Siam. The main body of people took nine days to reach Tavoy, having had to hack through a bamboo jungle for two days and climb two peaks, each of four thousand to five thousand feet. It had taken the group a fortnight to escape and they arrived in a terrible state. But at least they were free.

The morning after Ayer's announcement at the dance, Josiah Crosby telephoned my father to say that a Japanese task force had been sighted off the coast of Indo-China heading for Siam and the

Malayan Peninsula, but nevertheless he told my father to continue business as usual. A train was being organised for the 9th December to take people to Chieng Mai and then on to Chiang Rai on the borders of the Shan State of Burma. The train was unable to leave the station and at 2 o'clock in the afternoon of 8th December, Mother watched Japanese troops coming down Sathong Road with twigs covered in leaves stuck in their helmets as camouflage. They came up the drive and locked the doors so that my parents and Jon were imprisoned in their own house. One soldier who spoke broken English threatened to shoot anyone leaving. Father was most anxious to leave our house, Mamoi, as Japanese troops were in our garden watching the American Embassy next door while it was being pillaged. Any unauthorised person approaching the Embassy was shot. On the 11th December my brother Jonathon was allowed to have tea with Joanna Streatfield to celebrate her fourth birthday.

After a week my parents were able to leave Mamoi and drove to the Williams's house nearby, taking a few of their belongings in the car, and the three of them stayed there until the Siamese moved them to an internment camp. Meanwhile Fay's mother, Dorothy Williams, fled to the Standard Bank, where presumably she thought she would be safe. While all this was going on, Jon's Ayah stayed with the family; as a Siamese, she was free to come and go as she pleased so could bring in food and other provisions. Father buried all whisky and alcohol of any kind in the garden as the Japanese soldiers became particularly belligerent when they had had too much to drink. My parents had a teak box full of valuables, the lid of which had father's initials printed on the wood. One day a Swedish friend visited my parents; after planing off the initials he removed the box and took it to the Swedish compound in Bangkok for safety, but inevitably my parents were never to see it or the contents again.

Jon fell ill and as there was no English doctor they called in a German doctor who they knew well. "We are supposed to be at war and if I look after Jon who is going to pay me?" said the doctor. Jon was taken to hospital. My mother had a great deal of valuable jewellery, which she asked Ayah Lamduan to take to the Swiss Embassy, but they refused to accept it. Ayah's cousin somehow got to know about the jewellery and stole it, which upset my mother as much of it was of great sentimental value, having been given to her by her father. Most of the jewellery consisted of cut and uncut rubies given to my grandfather in payment for medical services rendered. Apart from some beautiful ruby rings and a necklace, Mother had a diamond brooch and various other items that she treasured.

On 23rd December at 2.30 in the morning, a truck full of Siamese soldiers, took mother and father to the University of Moral and Political Science, situated on the Menam River near one of the bridges and close to the Royal Palace.

The university rooms had been altered into a collection of partitioned cubicles ten feet high, sixteen feet long, and just over ten feet wide, each designed to house a family, however large or small. Each had soldiers' beds, and mattresses to sleep on, but the latter were full of fleas. Latrines and showers were in sheds outside the main building. Thanks to Ayah, father was able to buy two new beds and mattresses. By the 28th December there were one hundred and forty eight male and fifty two female internees, including children. Three weeks after Christmas, Jon, aged six, returned from hospital in an army truck guarded by armed enemy troops. The Siamese were responsible for looking after the inmates of the camp, and for the catering, while Japanese troops patrolled the outside of the building, which had been surrounded with a five-foot wooden fence topped with barbed wire which cut off the view of the river. Fortunately, my father had some money which he gave to Ayah, who used it to obtain essentials that they needed in the camp. Ayah, who was always trustworthy, would buy eggs which she would bring in secreted under straw. Mother would poach these on an electric iron turned upside down.

Mother remembers that food consisted almost always of sticky rice, which was terrible, or purple rice, which was quite tasty. Coffee, which was vile, was made by the Siamese caterers from roasted rice; bread, which was very coarse, was also made from rice and made Mother very ill. Stewed buffalo meat was sometimes supplied for lunch, and also the occasional banana. Ayah managed to obtain a pack of powdered milk from somewhere and also other foods from time to time, at great risk to her personal safety. If the Japanese had discovered she was smuggling in food she would have been shot. Jon was ill most of the time as he suffered from chronic colitis and Father was prone to dysentery from which he had suffered after many years in the East.

Twice daily Japanese troops entered the building to hold a roll call during which they threatened to rape the women and to kill the men.

All books were removed except for the Bible. My parents managed to hide a copy of 'The Innkeeper's Diary' and 'The Worst Journey in the World.' Other internees were also able to secrete the odd book. These books were read and re-read time and time again until they literally fell to pieces. 'The Seven Pillars of Wisdom' was particularly popular.

On the 29th December, Siamese police took father back home to Mamoi to see if there was anything he would like to keep. The house had been ransacked by the Japanese and the only thing father was able to save was a volume of Keats's poetry, which he took with him. By very good fortune someone gave father a load of wood, some nails and a hammer with which he was able to construct a makeshift desk and a new bed for himself. He constructed the bed to fit on top of the battered wardrobe to keep it out of the way during the day.

Once a day each family was supplied with one small bucket of cold water in which they were supposed to do all their washing. On one side of my parents' cubicle lived Mr. and Mrs. Streatfield in their cubicle, and on the other side a man who went mad. The Japanese did not understand why he had gone mad so they suspended him over his charpoy, a bed, and set it alight. He was badly burnt, then released, but eventually, as a result, of his burns he died. A number of internees went mad and when this happened the Japanese troops would first tie them to a post, break their legs and then put them to death. Mother had had a half share in a racehorse named Sai Sunee which was stabled with two other racehorses. The Japanese set fire to the building and all perished.

On 25th January 1942 Siam officially declared war on Britain and America. By 4th February 1942 there were two hundred and forty British internees at the camp where my parents were, the new arrivals mainly coming from the Trocadero Hotel, where they had been detained. Among the internees were a group of American missionaries who were always cheerful and kept up the spirits of the other internees very successfully. Meanwhile the United States authorities had been negotiating through Switzerland for the release of their civilian prisoners in Bangkok. On 29th June the American internees left for Saigon and freedom, arranged through Mr. Siegenthaler, the Swiss Consul, who was looking after British and American interests.

Mother's race horse

Mother read 'The Wind in the Willows' to the children. Nobody enquired where the book had been 'found'. Father meanwhile tried to teach the older children algebra and other subjects. On 28th April 1942, the British University lecturers put on 'A Midsummer Night's Dream', which was very much enjoyed; this was followed two months later by 'The Merchant of Venice', also excellent. Mother had to go to the Chulalongkorn hospital, with acute sciatica, for a few days. Worst of all was the sheer boredom: there was nothing to do but wait and worry. Of particular concern to Mother and Father was what had happened to me. Had I been caught in Sumatra? Or had the Bombay Burma Trading Corporation managed to get me out in time? Was I in fact alive or had I died during a possible evacuation? Father was never to know.

With so many housed in a rather restricted area there was bound to be friction from time to time. Mother offered to take care of David Sparrow, aged eleven, while his parents sorted out their problems but fortunately it never became necessary. Two single ladies refused to share a room together, but with the aid of the Rev. Eagling, an American, and the General Committee, this problem was also solved. Various internees had to go to the Chulalongkorn Hospital for treatment. There were numerous air raids by the Allies but most of the bombs landed in the Chinese quarter, which was very regrettable. None landed near the camp. By now all were getting thinner due to the poor diet. Children developed boils, skin eruptions and prickly heat, which easily became septic.

It was on the 4th August 1942 that permission was at last granted for any remaining British diplomats to leave, again thanks to the Swiss Consul. There were thirty five free places. As most of the diplomats had already left, three very sick men, and women with children under the age of twelve, were also allowed to go. Among the twelve diplomats were Mr. and Mrs. Streatfield. After a tearful goodbye Mother and Jon, along with the other evacuees, were taken, standing together in a truck, to the docks where a Siamese coastal steamer, the Valaya, was to take them to Saigon. As the truck drove through the camp gates there was a particularly poignant moment for my mother which brought tears to her eyes. Ah Fong our 'boy', had left my parents' employ shortly before the Japanese declared war, to work for an American. Father took on another Chinese 'boy' who, although willing, was quite hopeless, and Mother kept cursing him for his inefficiency. As the truck was driven from the camp this Chinese 'boy' was standing at the corner of the road with tears rolling down his cheeks and on seeing my mother he held up a cardboard box full of cakes for her to take. Unfortunately, he was too far away, and she could not take the box.

It was to be the last time they were to see my father. He was given a lethal injection administered by a Japanese orderly in August 1944 and witnessed by the Chairman of the General Committee Mr. Eric W. Deane. When eventually released at the end of the war Mr. Deane told my Mother that he, and another member of the General Committee, had had the unenviable job of witnessing the deaths of all ten of the British subjects who had died in camp, including my father.

The internees who sailed on the ship were placed on deck. The voyage took five days. Each was supplied with a small bucket of salt water to wash in during the morning and a small bucket of fresh water to drink. Food consisted of a meagre bowl of rice and curried fish once a day. They all slept on deck wherever they could find a spot to lie down. On arrival at Saigon, they were transferred to a Japanese liner, the Tatuta Maru, 17,000 tons and very fast, now

The Tatuta Maru

converted into a hospital ship, with red crosses painted on the hull and on deck. On board was the British Ambassador to Japan, Mr. Gore Booth who had sailed from Tokyo along with other members of his staff. The Tatuta Maru set sail from Saigon on 10th August 1942.

The Streatfields, like the other diplomats, were given cabins, while mother and Jon and the other internees were placed in steerage in the bowels of the ship where straw had been spread over the metal plates. Food was particularly poor, consisting mainly of inferior watery rice with buffalo stew, and very occasionally, curried fish. There were no dishes: everyone ate straight out of a bucket. Jon became very ill and delirious but a kindly secretary from the diplomatic service gave up her cabin to Jon for ten days while he recovered. A few of the babies died during the voyage.

Once a day, all internees were stripped naked by the Japanese guards, given a small bucket of water and told to go and wash. As by now everyone was ill with diarrhoea and the lavatories overflowing it meant they had to walk through sewage to get to the wash area and back, while the guards looked on, jeering and taunting, saying that the Japanese would win the war. Mother also became very ill but managed to survive until they reached Lourenço Marques, in Portuguese East Africa.

The Tatuta Maru docked at Lourenco Marques on the 27th August 1942. Exchange of internees did not start until 30th August, when Japanese women and children arrived from Britain. The exchange was strictly regulated: the number disembarking down one gangway had to equal the number of Japanese boarding the ship up a different gangway.

By now Jon was very ill again with dysentery and had to be taken off on a stretcher. Once on land, both mother and Jon were taken care of by the Red Cross and supplied with clothes and good food. On the 8th September the internees boarded the El Nil, a yacht that had once belonged to King Farouk, now acting as a hospital ship, with red crosses painted on deck and hull. Mother telegraphed the Bombay Burma Trading Corporation in Bombay for some money, which they sent for her to collect at Cape Town. When they reached South Africa, Mother was able to buy winter coats. From Cape Town, the El Nil sailed to the Canary Islands where she stopped to refuel, and then on up the west side of Ireland, around the north and then south, arriving at Liverpool on 9th October.

My Uncle Larry was there to meet mother and Jon off the ship as soon as it had docked; it was 7pm and he took them to the Adelphi Hotel. The following day they drove to Bedfordshire and stayed with Larry and Joan for Christmas. During this time Mother went to see her father in hospital at Guildford, where he died at the age of sixty-seven, ten days after mother had arrived back in England.

The S.S. El Nil, 1942